PAUSE

PAUSE

The *Power* of *Parenting* (and Living) with *Calm Connection*

Alice Hanscam
PCI Certified Parent Coach®

ISBN: 153755414X
ISBN 13: 9781537554143
Library of Congress Control Number: 2016915475
CreateSpace Independent Publishing Platform
North Charleston, South Carolina

A few words about PAUSE from others...

"Practicing PAUSE has shifted my focus from being reactive and trying to 'fix' my kids' problems or unwanted behaviors, to finding calmness in myself first so that I am able to connect with my child and listen to his/her needs. It is my go-to solution when my parenting skills fall through. That little bit of self-care gives me the strength to create better connections with my kids."

Debbie Whitecar, parent

"PAUSE is a peaceful existence in respect I never knew as a kid and am glad I can give to mine. My stepdaughter now *knows* that I will sit with her in all of her tumultuous feelings and help her get through them."

D. R., parent

"As a wife, mother, grandmother, and thirty-year elementary school teacher, I am strongly convinced that taking time to PAUSE has saved many relationships in my life. Most importantly it has helped me to reinvest into my family and thirty-two-year marriage. Pausing has increased my 'Self-Care Savings Account' abundantly. I no longer feel drained at the end of the day but instead inspired to give more."

Patty C., wife, parent, grandparent, and educator

"The biggest difference PAUSE has made for me was lessening the intense reactivity I experienced when triggered by my children. I found myself engaging in higher-quality interactions, and feeling less guilt and shame about how I parented, enjoying calm connection with my kids more and more. I also found that PAUSE gave me a greater ability to recognize joy in challenging parenting moments. Yes, all that from a simple PAUSE."

Nikki Polk, parent

"My work at pausing and then connecting calmly and quietly with my boys has allowed me to let go of trying to control the eye rolling, back talk, and BIG-GIANT feelings and instead think about what is really happening and what my boys' needs are right now. With a PAUSE I've discovered things to escalate less, my boys to think more, and all of us to reconnect respectfully and way more productively. I feel less guilty and stressed as a parent and understand my boys so much better!"

Dominique Brooks, Mom of two busy boys

"Seeing my son feeling hurt, sad, or frustrated, my gut reaction had been to jump in and make it all better, make the tears go away. PAUSE has taught me to step back, take a deep breath, and do my best to be a calm, reassuring presence and guide as he navigates his own way through big feelings. Even as he's slowly become more comfortable with his own emotions, I've proudly witnessed him purposefully engage as a soothing presence for others in times of stress."

Theresa Perez, parent

A few words about PAUSE from others...

"PAUSE allows me to be more mindful as a parent—to reflect and then reconnect calmly with my son whenever we struggle. And as I've gotten stronger at creating a PAUSE and leading with calm connection, I've noticed how conflicts with my son have lessened and my own awareness of what triggers me, of what I need to work on within myself, has grown. Reconnect and repair—both within myself and with my son. That is what PAUSE is doing for me."

Sharmi, parent

Dedication

To my family and all the parents, friends, and colleagues who have given me the opportunity to learn and grow alongside them.

To the Parent Coaching Institute for a transformative year that has brought me greater joy, confidence, and grace in all that I do.

To Hal Runkel and his book ScreamFree Parenting, *for bringing PAUSE into my life, changing it in profound and beautiful ways.*

Thank you.

Contents

In the Beginning...

I'm sure you know the drill—buttons pushed, kids not listening, fighting in the backseat of the car. Late for school, work, and anything else that requires everyone being ready to go on time. Sassing, back talking, eye rolling, whining, door slamming. And how about that frustrating "last word"? You know, when you have a child who is ultragood at getting in the last word, and it drives you nuts because you want (and feel you deserve because you ARE the adult...) the last word too? That was my daughter and me.

Or maybe you have the teen who is lost in their digital devices and offers up no words at all. That can really get a parent anxious. Or how about the tantrums by both toddlers and teens? Those teen tantrums caught me by surprise. Ever have a sobbing high-schooler in your lap? I have, and it was tough—all those BIG feelings pouring out of an adult-sized child. Really tough. And then there's the yelling, the bribing, the rushing to make everyone just STOP and listen and behave. Right *now*. Oh yes, I've been there too.

And then there's the guilt you feel as things just disintegrate... everyone melting down—including you. I know it well, for I've had my share of it—the guilt over being a lousy parent because I totally lost it with my child...or the heat rising in me as I thought, "I'm RIGHT, and they need to LISTEN." Those mornings filled with angst and rush and the push-push-push to get out the door...and everyone ultimately leaving upset—those were especially guilt-ridden for me, for I'd spend the entire day wishing for a do-over...wishing to reconnect and make sure my child wasn't upset anymore...hitting myself over the head for letting things get so out of hand that we parted mad at each other... feeling miserable all day long.

And really, I was just tired of arguing. I wanted to feel better. I wanted my children to feel better. And most important, I wanted our *relationships* to feel better—to be healthy and happy and calm. It was overwhelming at times.

Enter PAUSE. What a breath of fresh air. I first learned of the power of pausing through a favorite parenting book of mine— *ScreamFree Parenting* by Hal Runkel.[1] I began to practice it in my relationships, with my coaching clients, in my everyday life. I shared it with you in my first book, *Parenting Inspired; Finding Grace in the Chaos, Confidence in Yourself, and Gentle Joy along the Way.* I now bring it to you all on its own, for PAUSE has been the most positively influential "tool" for me and for many, many others: friends, colleagues, clients, family. Writing and then sharing *Parenting Inspired* with many of you has shown me just how essential pausing is for living well. There is so much more to be shared about the power of pausing and the calm connection that follows…hence this book focused entirely on what PAUSE is, how to use it, how to strengthen it, how it can change your life. If you want to focus on one thing that you can be guaranteed will create positive change in your life—a calmer self and household, healthier and more positive relationships, and deeper connections to yourself and to others—then I encourage you to focus on pausing.

It changes lives. It changed mine and continues to do so in sometimes surprising ways. I first saw the results of PAUSE when it began deintensifying heated moments with my teen daughter, allowing us both to cool off. Slowly and over time, yes, but it worked. With PAUSE growing stronger within me, I could stay calmer no matter how she chose to behave. With Mom calmer, daughter began to calm. And now we were connecting from a more peaceful place, able to listen more carefully to each other and to collaborate, cooperate, and be creative with ideas and solutions to any conflicts or other issues that arose. Anger, sadness, frustration, and guilt were replaced with *calm connection*. What a relief to not move through the day in a reactive mode, arguing and frustrated. What a gift to our relationship. Eight years later, our relationship has thrived and continues to grow in positive ways. Your relationships with your children can too.

But that's not where pausing ended for me, nor for many others who have continued to focus on it. As I got better and better at using PAUSE to calm down when I felt my buttons being pushed and the heat rising, I noticed some things. I noticed how I started to feel more relaxed in general, more aware of how I felt, how others were feeling. I became clearer about what I wanted and needed...both in my relationships with others and in everyday, seemingly "little" moments—such as when I had to decide what to make for dinner (some nights that made all the difference in how I and, as a result, my family felt!), or when I had to choose whether or not it was necessary (or healthy!) to squeeze in one more activity despite the pleading of my kids. Then I realized I was taking more time for me—making deposits into my "Self-Care Savings Account." I felt better, inside out. Patience ruled. My sense of humor improved (to my husband's relief...☺), the time I spent with my girls became increasingly more satisfying and joyful.

PAUSE took me even further. Because I felt less rushed and more relaxed throughout my day (no matter the number of activities my girls had or how crazy my work schedule was), I found I was able to be more focused and present—to my girls, to others, to all that I was doing, and especially to myself. Things that used to stress me out (like tired and cranky kids AND a million things to get done!) began to be enjoyable, or at least tolerable. Life flowed with greater ease. I even felt less tired, even though a good night's sleep was a rare event. Oh, and the joy! It seemed to begin to weave its way through every single day—in little ways at first, and then more noticeably over time. Joy—just think what could be different if this was your foundation from which you parented each day!

Here's the coolest thing that PAUSE has done for me. It's led to a calm connection with *myself* that continues to grow and has become the foundation for my parenting and living well. Pausing, and the calm connection that follows, has me feeling centered and at ease. It has allowed me to actually welcome uncomfortable situations, the chaos of raising children and the accompanying BIG feelings, the uncertainty that any change can bring—whether it is illness that throws plans out the window, a job loss and family move, the disruption of failing appliances or cars, or simply unexpected homework that has you and your child scrambling.

I find, as I grow my ability to PAUSE and let calm connection lead the way, I am now more available to everyone and everything in my life. In lovely ways. In deeply satisfying ways. In no longer feeling stretched-too-thin-or-overwhelmed ways. And another cool thing about PAUSE? Even when things go south (and they do!), the calm connection I've grown through pausing has me re-centering more quickly, able to move through the yuck with a bit more grace and confidence, actually noticing and appreciating the gifts and opportunities it provides. With calm connection leading the way, I can see chaos, conflict, and challenge for what they are—opportunities for growth. Talk about making the yuck something to actually welcome and appreciate! Really. Welcome and appreciate. Imagine doing that right now as you face your current challenge with your children. Imagine what could be different for you and for them if you were actually opening your arms to this challenge and inviting it in, feeling comfortable, appreciative, and on the lookout for the positive growth it has to offer. Imagine feeling absolutely certain that you are the calm, in-charge, confident parent your child needs. Now what could be different for you and your children?

Calm connection. This is the power that PAUSE brought into my life. It can do the same for you. You can embrace it as a "simple" tool to help you move through conflict with your child, or you can take it further and discover the greater gifts it brings. Either way, it can change your relationships in positive and powerful ways. And it can change your life. It continues to change mine.

Perhaps you are coming to this book desperate to stop yelling at your children, or to stop feeling so crummy about how each day unfolds or how negative interactions with your child leave you feeling. Perhaps you are really struggling to find a way to calm yourself down, to create the connection with your child that leaves you feeling good—truly good—about your relationship, about your child and who he or she is becoming, about yourself as a parent. Or maybe you feel pretty confident with your parenting skills but would give anything to bring more ease and joy into the busy life that engulfs you and your family. Maybe you find yourself saying things like, "If I only had more time…If only we COULD…Maybe tomorrow…maybe." And off you run again on another round of activities, work, grabbing take-out for dinner or microwaving left-overs, snatching bits of time to wipe away tears, zip coats, help with homework, rescue your toddler from yet another attempt at climbing up the shelving, switch the laundry, wade through the piles of paperwork, wish your teen would find a better time to talk than midnight when you have finally collapsed into bed. No matter your reasons for picking up this book, know that you have plenty of company in your challenges and frustrations. Plenty!

Let this book inspire you to continue the hard work of parenting well. Find that calm connection through the strengthening of your pause muscle.[2] (That's what it really is, a muscle—a concept I embraced from *ScreamFree Parenting*.) Let it show you how to use PAUSE at its basic level, allowing you to calmly handle those button-pushing moments (and days), or let it inspire you to take PAUSE deeper, to completely transform your way of being. Enjoy and take encouragement and inspiration from the stories and examples from parents just like you. **Let this book gently guide you as you grow stronger in the power of parenting with calm connection.** Let it bring you to greater peace, more ease, and real joy in all your relationships. You and your children are worth it.

Let it change your life.

Alice
PCI Certified Parent Coach®
ScreamFree Certified Leader

PAUSE

The Power of Parenting (and Living) with Calm Connection

Let's Begin with a Story...

Rachel cringed as another round of tantrums began from her preschool daughter, Sarah. She had relented to Sarah's pleas that morning and taken her to a favorite play place once again, even though Rachel knew from experience that, without a doubt, there would be at least one exhausting fit to deal with. And she was right. It came after Sarah used the potty—washing hands could last forever! Rachel could feel the tension within her climb as she tried convincing Sarah to finish quickly so that they could go play some more. Sarah would have none of it—"NO! I'm not DONE." Bribing Sarah didn't work, and threatening her that she'd have no more time to play fell on deaf ears. Finally, Rachel had enough of her daughter not obeying. She turned off the faucet and pulled Sarah out of the bathroom. Sarah screamed and kicked as Rachel—frustrated, mortified, and fuming—told her, "You aren't minding me, so we are going home!" The fighting, the tears, and the screaming (and what felt like all eyes upon them) persisted all the way out to the car. By

the time Sarah was buckled in—an enormous accomplish-
ment with a writhing four-year-old—Rachel AND Sarah were
exhausted. As Rachel drove home, tears streamed down her
face. "Why can't she just behave? If she'd only listen. I feel
so embarrassed…" The ride home was miserable as Sarah
moved from screams to sobs to a fitful sleep. Upon arriving
home, things just never got better—Sarah got woken up too
soon as she was pulled out of her car seat, the tantrum con-
tinued, Rachel enforced a time-out, and they both felt out of
sorts for the rest of the afternoon.

Whew. Quite the story—and probably a familiar one for you. If you haven't confronted a tantrumming toddler or preschooler lately, maybe it is a story of homework and nagging and resistance that defines your most frustrating moments. I spent a lot of time looking over my teen's shoulder, asking over and over again, "What have you gotten done? How can you possibly focus on your work while messaging your friends and following Facebook at the same time? What did your teacher say? When do you plan on tackling…?" On and on I'd persist with what quickly became a one-way conversation, resulting in both of us getting increasingly mad and my daughter becoming more resistant and even yelling at me to leave her alone. The day she shouted, "Mom, if you don't stop nagging me, I will quit doing any of my homework!" caused me to stop and think. My intent in what I thought was "checking in" with her (a.k.a. nagging) was for her to DO her homework (my way…without distraction…right now…) Here she was telling me that all my efforts to make sure she did her job of being a good student were wasted—that I was nagging her to death and sending her down the road of choosing to do just what I had hoped to avoid: no homework accomplished and becoming a failure as a student. Yikes!

Enter the Power of PAUSE.

⸺✸⸺

What does it mean to PAUSE?

"Pause, take a moment to find a place of calm within you, think about what it is you want the most in the situation, then respond based on this, rather than react to the emotions or circumstance of the moment." [1]

Hal Runkel, *ScreamFree Parenting*

⸺✸⸺

Here's the deal. When we learn to create a PAUSE—a space between stimulus (my daughter talking back to me or a four-year-old's tantrum) and response (how we decide to respond to the behavior)—we can take control of ourselves and choose with intention and purpose just what we really want to communicate. As a result, our response can be one that is relationship-building rather than relationship-depleting. One that is calm and clear rather than angry and reactive. One that still says NO if necessary, but is communicated with the respect that our calm can provide and our anger never can.

The key here? **To take control of ourselves.**[2] So often when we get into these reactive situations with our children, our intent is to control THEM, to *make* them do or not do something. Pretty tough thing to accomplish, controlling someone. I remember trying so, so hard to get my three-and-a-half-year-old daughter to STOP hurting our cat—to *make* her only use gentle hands. The more I tried to control her actions—ultimately by getting madder and more frustrated and actually resorting to yanking her away to a time-out—the rougher my preschooler was on our poor kitty. The problem with trying to control another is that it's impossible. No matter our efforts, they can always say NO. And when they say NO, we try harder and harder to make them do whatever it is we want them to do, because their NO pushes our button. We get more frustrated, our voices get louder, we feel angrier. All my daughter learned from my futile attempts at making her be gentle, was how to make me mad. Her attention was on me and my reactivity rather than on herself and how to be with our cat.

I learned, eventually, that I needed to *first calm and take control of myself.* When I paused and took the moment I needed, I considered what I really wanted—for my daughter to learn how to be gentle with others (animals and people alike!). I thought about what has worked for her to learn in other situations (repetition and lots of practice), I was then able to let patience step up as I repeatedly showed her what "gentle pats" looked like, gave her more positive attention, and removed the CAT from the room (instead of her) when she was unable to be gentle. Eventually my calmer connection with my daughter and our cat paid off. Gentle hands were used, less negative attention was acted out on our kitty, and cool heads prevailed. My daughter's attention was now more on herself and what *she* was doing (rather than on my behavior), allowing her to be in charge of HERSELF in positive ways—just what I had really wanted all along. As for kitty, the amazing thing was that, despite the rough treatment early on, she became my daughter's sidekick for years to come!

**PAUSE allows us to focus on
and take control of *ourselves* first, so that we
CAN positively influence our children.**

We cannot control our children, but we certainly can influence them—quite profoundly, as a matter of fact. Controlling means doing whatever it takes to *make sure* that our children think, feel, and act in exactly the way *we* need them to, no matter how *they* feel about it. This often leaves kids with only two choices: obeying out of fear of being in trouble (which can lead to them resenting us), or rebelling against us (leaving *us* angrier and more resentful toward them). Over time, this is exhausting and relationship-depleting... not what any of us intend as we do our best to guide our children.[3]

When we try to control our children, we often do so with good intentions...but it is also a result of our anxiety over being a good parent, our need to feel in control of a child who can often act quite OUT of control, our desire to avoid feeling embarrassed, and **our wish to parent well and feeling a lack of confidence in just how to do so.** The mom at the play place wanted desperately for her daughter to stop with the hand washing so that playing wouldn't be short-changed and cause a tantrum. That way Mom wouldn't feel embarrassed and instead would feel more in control. I wanted to make sure my teen was a good student so that she would thrive in school and I could feel like a good parent for raising such a smart daughter. I wanted to make sure my preschooler was gentle with our cat so that she wouldn't hurt her, but I ALSO wanted to feel like the good parent who has a child who knows how to treat animals (and listens to me!).

Our need for our children to choose behavior we want (so WE can feel better, calmer, more able to manage and be the good parent we so desperately want to be) often leads to creating more of the behavior we are trying to avoid—all because our kids are now way more focused on us and thinking about how we feel than on their own behavior and how it makes *them* feel. Whew. And with our children's attention on us and our needs rather than on themselves, it displaces their ability to learn more about themselves—how they feel, what they like or don't like, can or cannot do, need or don't need, etc.—making it more difficult to grow the confident, capable, independent future adults we hope for.

Pausing is all about creating the space (however brief) that we need to make sure we calm ourselves, take care of our own anxiety and upset feelings, get a bit clearer on what it is we really want in this situation (whether it is compliance in the moment or a long term vision of helping our child learn a bit more about managing him or herself well) and then stepping back into a situation with *calm connection leading the way.* It is shifting our attention from worrying so much about how our child decides to behave to focusing on how *we* want to behave in order to positively influence our child—something we *can* do.

PAUSE allows us to acknowledge our anxiety over a situation and gently calm this anxiety. Now there's a bit of essential self-care! We can then consider how best to help our children (in this particular situation) grow their capable and competent selves so they can more likely decide *on their own* (truly the mark of independent, capable souls) to make good decisions and behave in positive, productive ways—to listen, cooperate, share, be respectful and kind, take responsibility for themselves...

Or PAUSE may simply allow us to understand how we can best stop what might be unsafe behavior in such a way that our child's attention is on his behavior and feelings rather than on our upset. PAUSE allows us to be *in control of ourselves* no matter what our child decides to do. What a way to role-model what it's like to be a respectful and mature adult—something we intend for our children to eventually become ☺. What a way to communicate, "You are safe with me; we will be okay." What a way to build trust...to communicate "You can count on me." What a way to build relationships in positive and meaningful ways. And now our children will be more likely to turn to us as the resource they need as they grow. That's something I believe we all want to be for our children—the resource they turn to and listen to.

What actually *is* a PAUSE?

PAUSE "looks" many different ways. Hal Runkel likes to see it as pushing the pause button on a remote control[4]—something we all have plenty of around our homes, making it easier to remember to use

PAUSE. Or, as another parent described it, PAUSE is imagining you are wearing all your shirt buttons inside out so that they are unavailable to be pushed. Maybe you see yourself taking one long deep breath and creating a space—physically and perhaps mentally. I like to see PAUSE in my mind's eye as a space filled with light—rather like a bubble around myself or around the child pushing my button. Yet another parent I know likes to draw a pause button on her hand, often engaging her kids to help push it. Now that brings a bit of lightheartedness to the challenging moments ☺.

No matter how you see PAUSE, or what you do to create one (more on this in the following chapter), you will always feel its positive impact. Even if you just *pretend* you are feeling calmer (maybe still churning away on the inside), an amazing thing happens. Your body relaxes a bit and your brain begins to actually process all those churning thoughts. You move away from the reactive "I don't want to feel embarrassed!" or other anxiety-driven self-talk and toward a consideration of just what it is you want your child to have the opportunity to learn—"Okay. She's struggling with something difficult...I can be patient and see this through." And even with just a small bit of relaxation and a brain that can think even an iota, you can make **a positive difference.**

**PAUSE creates the space we need to gain
clarity and confidence so we can parent with the
power of calm connection.**

The Safe Place of PAUSE

The more we exercise our pause muscle and create a calmer space within us, the more our brains can think with clarity and purpose. Now we tend to move more slowly, calmly, even gently. And at times of real safety issues when our speed is essential? We find we can still exhibit (maybe not actually *feel*) a sense of calm control *despite* our adrenaline pumping wildly through us. Think about the classic story of a young child dashing into the street chasing her ball. In this situation, as we respond with the necessary speed for safety, PAUSE gives us clarity on how we want to behave and speak so our little one can more likely learn to stop when we say stop, to stay put on the sidewalk, to ask an adult for help. The more we can slow ourselves down (perhaps mentally if not physically, as in this example) and respond from a sense of calm, the better able we are to really connect with our child. *This calm connection is what positively influences them*—it communicates respect, understanding, acceptance, an "I'm listening and what you say is important to me" message. Another key result of our slower, calmer, gentler approach? **It feels safe to a child**. With this feeling of safety, children can get less worked up—and this allows their brains to actually process what we are saying and showing to them—*what it is we intend for them to learn*. What a way to positively influence our child! And in those moments of danger, it becomes a gift to us, as well, for the adrenaline pumping through us, stirring up our anxiety and fear, actually lessens…and now we are more able to be the safe, calm place for our child (and us!) to learn from.

I remember the story of a mother I coached whose two-and-a-half-year-old son raced toward a partially frozen lake, full speed ahead. She ran—faster than she ever felt possible—and caught up with him, stopped and wrapped her arms around him, and breathed (PAUSE!), then said in a shaky but quiet voice, "It's not safe to be down here without Mommy…" She acted quickly and calmly despite the adrenaline pumping through her. What could have resulted in a complete meltdown (understandably) for both Mom and son—Mom yelling out of fear for him to never do that again and her son becoming a puddle of tears or a tantruming toddler—became, instead, a relationship-building experience with a child able to learn a bit more about self-management, about the danger of half-frozen ponds…and about being able to count on his mother. All because of a PAUSE and the power of calm connection.

This is why PAUSE is so powerful—it influences challenging, negative, even scary situations in such a way that they can ultimately strengthen relationships—they become relationship-building rather than relationship-depleting. The calm we project (whether we actually feel it or not) as a result of PAUSE allows children to feel **safe and secure.** *They can now count on us to keep it together no matter how they feel.* Now we can feel more connected and our children can "hear" our confidence in them. What a difference that can make. What a way to empower our children to learn from their experiences.

PAUSE in Action—Story Time!

Let's return to our story and see what unfolds as Rachel uses a PAUSE to create calm connection with little Sarah...a do-over with a PAUSE in place:

> *Rachel cringed at the potential of another round of tan-trums from her preschool daughter, Sarah. She had relented and taken her daughter to a favorite play place once again, even though Rachel knew, without a doubt, there would be at least one exhausting fit to deal with. And she was right! It came following using the potty—washing hands could last forever with Sarah—and Rachel could feel the pressure climb as she tried convincing Sarah to be done so they could go play some more. Sarah would have none of it—"NO! I'm not DONE." Rachel sighed. "Here we go again!" she thought. She paused by taking a deep breath. Then she considered what she knew usually worked well to help her daughter move through these experiences with a bit more grace (something she had plenty to draw from, for they seemed to happen often throughout*

each day ☺). She began by letting Sarah know she could wash for another minute and then it would be time to be all done. Rachel knew from past successes how important it was for her daughter to have a sense of control via knowing just what to expect.

The minute passed, and Sarah still resisted finishing—water play is such fun for four-year-olds! Rachel, who continued her PAUSE by staying quiet and focusing on relaxing during that extra minute, calmly followed through with her promise of one more minute and reached over to help turn off the faucet. Screams and tears burst forth from Sarah. Mom then took a few more deep breaths, reminding herself that these were tough experiences for preschoolers and that she wanted Sarah to discover she could handle the disappointment of being all done with something fun, that being disappointed and mad was okay, and that Mom was someone she could count on to keep it together no matter how Sarah felt or behaved.

Rachel's breaths and encouraging self-talk helped her stay calm despite the fit from her daughter. She knew what needed to happen and with calm confidence gathered up her puddle-of-a-four-year-old as best she could, saying, "I know you wanted to wash for longer. It's disappointing when you have to be done with something fun." Rachel then took her out into the hall that led back to the play place and said, "Here's a good place to get your mad out. I will be right here, and when you've calmed down and feel ready, we can go play some more." Sarah continued with her MAD—yelling at her mom, lying on the floor kicking and crying.

A play place attendant appeared and asked, "Is everything okay?"

"Yes," said Rachel. "Sarah is feeling mad and disappointed that she had to be all done with washing up. When she is done getting her mad out, we'll head back to play."

And Rachel waited. (PAUSE...) Sarah eventually wound down, and Rachel stepped close saying, "I can see you are feeling calmer. Are you ready to go play a bit more?"

"YES!" her daughter exclaimed. And off they went, with Sarah zipping ahead saying, "Watch me, Mommy!" (Fours have an amazing power to flip from incredibly frustrating to wonderfully delightful ☺).

When it was time to head home, Rachel fully expected a total kicking and screaming meltdown once again. She was pleasantly surprised (and relieved!) to find that her daughter expressed her mad with her words and stomping feet: "I don't want to go. I LIKE it here...can we come back soon?"

With Rachel's ability to PAUSE and lead with calm connection, she found herself being a bit more playful with Sarah, joining in with the stomping, affirming "YES! Let's make plans to come back soon."

What could have been a rough transition became one filled with empathy and gentle humor (just what fours need lots of). Rachel effortlessly buckled Sarah into the car. They headed home, with conversation moving from all the fun at the play place to what the rest of their day would look like. After sharing a snack together at home, the afternoon unfolded unremarkably, with both Mom and Sarah enjoying the results of the calm connection PAUSE created.

See how impactful PAUSE and the power of creating calm connection can be? It ripples out in sometimes surprising (and wonderful) ways. Rachel discovered that her preschooler, rather than melting into a full-blown tantrum, was able to express her upset with words and stomping feet—a much more productive way for a preschooler to deal with upset feelings. Now Rachel no longer felt tense—allowing her to commiserate and stomp alongside her daughter, creating the very connection Sarah needed to feel more in control of HER feelings. This led them into an afternoon of relative ease—rather than one of anger, hurt feelings, and guilt.

I discovered that when I calmed myself down first before I worked with my preschooler to be kind with our cat, she *listened*. She began practicing her gentle pats—and felt quite proud of herself as kitty began to purr, which encouraged her further. Then she began to extend her gentle pats to others—such as her baby sister ☺—and responded more readily to my calm reminders to use her gentle hands. My *trust* in her ability to manage herself grew—and therefore her *ability* to manage herself grew as well. Cool, hmmm?

And my homework-nagging saga with my teen? I paused by leaving her room, taking some time to think about what I really wanted. This led me to the clarity that if she could communicate her plan for tackling her work, I could let go of checking in (a.k.a. nagging) on a regular basis. I reconnected with my daughter, let her know what I expected (a plan), gave her my promise to stop nagging, and then gave her the respect of space and time to focus on her work, her way. My daughter responded beautifully! She'd tell me her plan when I asked for it. I in turn worked hard at keeping myself out of her room. (More pausing was required via focusing on tasks—I sure accomplished a lot of little chores during those times!) As a result, her work was done well and in a timely fashion. My PAUSE, which allowed me to let go of controlling and step in with calm connection, led her to feel trusted and capable and confident in herself. Just what I REALLY wanted! The cool thing? She began, on her own, to seek me or her dad out for advice, brainstorming, or just for a bit of encouragement. Talk about feeling a deeper and more positive connection with our teen—and a teen taking responsibility for herself! What an amazing ripple-out effect of pausing.

———⚬⚬⚬———

Let's take a moment and reflect...
PAUSE allows you to:

- Focus first on yourself and take a moment to find a place of calm within you.
- Feel less anxious, embarrassed, mad, tense—you name it.
- Think about what you really want in the situation.
- Respond based on what you really want instead of react to the emotions or circumstance of the moment.
- Be in control of YOURSELF—what a way to be a positive role-model for your child!
- Feel clearer and more confident in how you respond.
- Let calm connection lead the way, communicating understanding *of*, respect *for*, and trust and confidence *in* your child.
- Influence your child in profoundly relationship-building and positive ways.
- Be the calm leader your child needs in order to learn and grow in healthy ways.

———⚬⚬⚬———

The Bigger Gifts of PAUSE...

Then there are the bigger gifts PAUSE and calm connection bring. As we get stronger with our pause muscle—truly calling upon it on a regular basis—*calm connection becomes the norm*. It begins to expand from the immediate impact of less intense conflict and more cooperation. The way we move through our day changes—we become more present, less frantic and overwhelmed; we feel more deeply connected with those we love and more meaningfully connected to others we meet throughout our day. You noticed it in the previous stories: how Rachel and Sarah could actually enjoy their afternoon together; how my teen grew in her ability to take responsibility for herself and began to see my husband and me as the resource for her we had always wanted to be; how my preschooler felt proud of her ability to interact with our kitty in ways that had the kitty wanting more—and left my little one feeling just a bit more confident and capable, influencing other areas of her life.

The bigger gifts of PAUSE include the real and meaningful connection with others *and ourselves* that occurs. *It is the power of both parenting and living with calm connection.* And "power" it is, for it ultimately infuses everything we do with ease, confidence, respect, trust, wonder, acceptance, compassion, and joy. With PAUSE, we can feel strong and steady and good—*balanced* no matter the chaos we find ourselves in. PAUSE helps you to trust, truly trust, that no matter what comes your way, *you will be okay.* It may be in time and after a lot of tears, but you know—from the inside out—that you will be okay.

What a gift PAUSE can bring beyond the initial calming of conflict! Now you are more likely going to find a way to welcome in the yuck that can (and will) happen in parenting (and life); you will be able to see it—live it—through the lens of appreciation and gratefulness. Even if the only thing you can be grateful for is another's gentle hug because you feel at a total loss. Even if the only thing you can appreciate is the warm bed you fall into each night or that you actually DID get loaded up into the car despite the screaming and kicking of your child. With this "lens of appreciation" that PAUSE and living with calm connection brings, what could have potentially left you depleted can now become affirming, energizing, even empowering.

That gentle hug when you felt at a total loss? It shores you up rather than being something to shrug off. Falling into your warm bed? It has you smiling a bit as you snuggle in, able to let go of the craziness of the day and welcome in the exhaustion that will have you sleeping well. Your heroic effort to get everyone loaded up in the car? With calm connection being a way of life, and seeing things through a lens of appreciation, you are more likely feeling the success of the moment, smiling a bit, letting your mind wander to what you are looking forward to—rather than dreading the incessant whining from the back seat. You now are more likely to engage with your children creatively and with more lightheartedness, perhaps singing or telling stories or just turning on music—letting go of whether they decide to cool their jets or not! Just think of how this can influence the rest of your day...or at least the drive in to school or work ☺.

This is the power of PAUSE. It brings calm connection, growing your ability to see all things from a far more affirming, empowering, lifting place. And we all need to be lifted...especially as we navigate the difficult journey parenting can be. Simply put, PAUSE *transforms relationships*. **Let's get started.** It's time to roll up our sleeves, to learn how to PAUSE and how to strengthen this muscle so you, too, can discover the gifts and reap the benefits of parenting and living with calm connection. PAUSE can bring joy to all that you do. What a gift for our children!

THIS **can be your story.**

PAUSE at its Basic

Those Button Pushing Moments...

Now that you know more about what PAUSE is and how calm connection can rule when it comes to parenting well and building relationships in positive ways, it's time to understand how to put PAUSE to work. Let's first see how it's used in those button-pushing, blood-pressure-accelerating, had-it-up-to-here moments. This is where PAUSE begins and calm connection can first emerge. Maybe one (or more!) of the following scenarios are familiar to you:

- You have five more minutes until everyone MUST be out the door if you are going to arrive at school and work on time. You are already running behind because your kids dragged themselves out of bed w-a-a-a-y too slowly that morning...and now the contents of their backpacks are strewn across the floor as they are chasing the dog up and down the stairs, screeching at the tops of their lungs...

- Your teen rolls her eyes at you and in THAT tone of voice says, "D-a-a-a-d! I already TOLD you...," then storms off to her room, slamming her door, emphasizing (as only teens can) that you didn't "get" what she was trying to tell you...

- You've got a three-year-old who has decided the car seat is evil and fights you every inch of the way. Limp arms and dragging feet are followed by an arching back and SCREAMS, leaving you wondering if you'll lose your hearing as you work hard to just get him IN and buckled safely…

- Here you go again; your kids are refusing to share and end up fighting. They start with a grab, a push, and then a "That's MINE!" It ends up with hitting, tears, and a "M-o-o-o-m! Make him STOP!"

- You sound like a broken record as you tell your child over and over and over again to do something, but she just continues to ignore you. Why can't she just LISTEN?!

- Your toddler just won't STOP throwing his blocks and then biting you when you try to stop him; or turning into a puddle of tears each time you say no to her; or pushing you away, kicking and screaming, when you try to help as he struggles to put on his OWN shoes…

- Homework is a long and weary struggle each evening because your children (a) refuse to do it, (b) do it only halfheartedly, or (c) feel obligated to do it to perfection…and if they don't succeed, they exclaim that they are failures (or throw it all out to start over once again, making it a v-e-r-y long and crabby evening…as my daughter used to do). Exhausting for everyone.

I'm sure you've lived at least some of these difficult scenarios (and maybe plenty of others), and I bet you remember how you felt the heat rise, how your stomach or jaw clenched, how perhaps your mind started a-whirling, or maybe you felt tense across the shoulders. Your self-talk was probably filled with, "Not *again*. When will they LEARN? They never listen, and I just don't know what to do. If I'd talked like that to *my* parents I'd have gotten a spanking and been grounded for LIFE. Arghhh!"

All these reminders that your button was pushed? They are important to tune in to, for they tell you it is time to PAUSE—**they are your "red flags" and are there to actually *help* you.** They tell you it is time to exercise your pause muscle, for if you don't, you already know what can unfold. As you get more and more anxious or angry, you REACT, and it might look like this:

- You totally lose your temper, yelling right back at your child, maybe even slamming a door or two yourself...not quite what you really intended to role-model!

- You threaten with often unreasonable consequences like "You'll be grounded for a month!" or "I'm going to take away your computer FOREVER!" or "If you don't quit, you'll never get to come here again!"

- You bribe your child with all manner of enticing things (like too many cookies as one dad I know found himself doing) or false promises to "get them to behave" such as "I'll let you watch all your favorite movies this weekend if you'll only..." or "If you just do (fill in the blank) I'll let you have as many friends as you'd like spend the night tomorrow..." Yet you *know* there is no way you'll let them watch TV all weekend long or let all those kids come over and wreak havoc all night long!

- You check out entirely by hiding out in the bathroom with a favorite book and hoping everything will just hurry up and solve itself...whew, that was easy! And then you wonder why your kids don't come to you as the resource you'd like to be for them—why would they, if all you do is hide or check out when the going gets tough?

- You plead with your child over and over and over to do whatever it is you want him to do, getting increasingly hot and reactive as he continues to ignore you...which is why you keep on pleading. Now *that* is exhausting—and rarely productive.

Typically, things settle down eventually (whew!), but you feel totally wiped out. Or maybe you feel terribly guilty. Or your child's anger toward you continues throughout the day. Maybe you find yourself dreading the next round of button-pushing interactions with them, sure to be coming right around the corner...dreading, because you really want it to be different, to go smoother, to feel better—and you just don't know how to make that happen.

PAUSE, at its basic, takes these trying moments and turns them into relationship-building moments. When we step back into a challenging scenario from a place of calm, we immediately deintensify it. The situation tends to spiral up less, and our child "hears" or senses our calm. This is key, as I mentioned earlier, **for it communicates to them they can count on us to keep it together no matter how they decide to behave.** It communicates our confidence in their ability to manage themselves. It leaves them feeling more safe and secure in our calm. It lets them grow their capable selves just a bit more and leaves them feeling a bit more heard and understood. And that goes a l-o-n-g way *toward* eventual cooperation and collaboration and *away* from resistance and reactiveness. *Calm connection begins to rule!*

When to PAUSE

Remember those red flag reminders your body presents you? Get to know them well—the heat, the clenching, the tenseness, the negative self-talk. As I said earlier, these physical reactions to your button being pushed are there to help you. They create an opportunity—with PAUSE in place—to learn a bit more about yourself, how you react to stress, and more importantly, **how you can change your reaction to a healthier, relationship-building response**. Noticing your "red flags" when your buttons are pushed is an opportunity for growth that comes your way many times a day as a parent—many! Just think of all the practice we get to strengthen that pause muscle of ours ☺. And it always gives you the chance to create a positive connection with your child that can, in time, make parenting easier.

How to PAUSE

So now you know to pay attention to how your body feels. Now you know that this is the moment when a PAUSE can truly begin to benefit you and your child. Now it's time to discover just what techniques work best for you to actually PAUSE.

Here are some things to think about that I explore with my coaching clients, parents who attend my workshops, and anyone else who is trying to parent more calmly and with more connection. Considering these will help you discover what works for you to PAUSE:

1. *Take a moment and think about a time you've felt especially good about how a conflict or challenge unfolded—or maybe about a potential conflict or challenge that surprised you because it actually didn't blow up.*

2. *Consider a time you felt good about how YOU behaved in a conflict with your child.*

3. *Take a moment and think about when you have felt calm despite your child totally losing it.*

Maybe it was bedtime last week—one night when your child actually listened and ran upstairs to brush teeth and put jammies on without the usual nagging or knock-down, drag-out fight. Or maybe it was today when you were both leaving school and you enjoyed a brief conversation with your child instead of having to pry them away from the playground in tears. Or perhaps you feel especially good about how the usual homework battle went recently—that even though your child *still* didn't get everything done before dinner, they were less upset, and you actually stayed reasonably calm the entire time (and dinner was on time as a result!). Perhaps it was a time you said *no* and meant it, and your child listened—the first time you said it! Maybe, if there is nothing that comes to mind with regards to parenting, it was a time you realized a disagreement with a coworker actually ended up with you both moving forward productively. Or a time when, despite a crazy traffic jam, you found yourself singing along with the radio and, rather than letting frustration take over, you actually enjoyed the extra time in your car.

It can be difficult coming up with these memories. It's often the tough times that really stand out for us and make it especially hard to think of anything else. I encourage you to keep thinking and reflecting. Look to right now, today, for something going better, for what is putting a smile on your face. Remember events such as holidays, vacations, or playing outside with your children. Conflicts are (sometimes!) more easily diffused or don't even come up when routines or locations are different. Think about those fun family trips—now it's no longer a struggle to get your kids going in the morning! Or maybe it was leaving the park one day. You were feeling especially good about and pleasantly exhausted with all the racing around you and your kids did. You found yourself totally okay with your kids' NOT wanting to leave and were able to get loaded up in the car with a sense of humor in place. Keep thinking! These memories will emerge…I promise ☺.

Once you have a few memories of experiences you felt good about, think about how YOU were feeling during these more successful moments. Were you feeling:

- Calmer, more matter-of-fact?
- Relieved? Relaxed?
- Connected to your child?

- More focused and present?
- In charge and in control?
- Lighter, with a sense of humor in place?
- Clear on just what needed to happen?
- Confident—in yourself, in your decision, in your child's abilities?
- Less concerned with the event in general—able to let go and go with the flow?
- Curious, rather than worried, about how things would unfold?
- Compassion or empathy for the person you were with (child or someone else)?

In the following space, list the feelings you experienced in these scenarios. Even if you can only write, "I was feeling better..." think about just what "better" means to you, write how it "looks." Maybe it "looked" like a child who cooperated, or it "looked" like you in a more relaxed state or feeling in control (because your child DID listen!). Maybe "better" translates to just getting out the door when you intended—and now you feel a bit more confident with your day starting out on the right track. Perhaps "better" meant when you finally got to work you felt totally focused on the project in front of you. Keep thinking about how you felt. Write this down, and then keep on reading! We are getting closer to just what works to PAUSE.

———— ✦ ————

At these times I felt...

———— ✦ ————

My next question for you is this:

What allowed you to feel calm, connected, a bit more relaxed, clear, confident, able to let go and go with the flow, to be matter-of-fact or to feel any of the other feelings you listed above?

In other words, why, in this particular scenario you thought of, were you *able* to feel calmer (which is typically the feeling that prevails)? This is where some parents will say, "Because my child listened to me!" And I will say, YES—but they listened to you because of the energy you gave off as you interacted with them. They listened better because you were calmer; you were calmer because they listened better. *Yet there is more to it.* Think about:

- **What thoughts were going through your head?** Perhaps something like, "This really isn't a big deal, we will get through it." Or "I know I can keep this going in the right direction!" Maybe it was "Breathe, breathe, breathe...he's only three/thirteen." Or maybe you were thinking "Look at him go! Pretty impressive, the energy he has!" or "Ha! I remember having the same fight with MY sister at her age!"

- **What were you actually doing physically?** Taking a few deep breaths? Counting to ten? Did you find yourself moving away from your child to go get something done in the other room—all the while hoping when you returned they will have done what you've asked? Maybe you realize you were next to your child, touching their shoulder. Perhaps you found yourself closing your eyes...biting your tongue...heading downstairs (like I used to do to go unload on my husband...☺). Or maybe you were just moving forward with whatever needed to be done with merely a shrug of your shoulders over the antics of your child.

Whatever you realize you did that actually let you stay a bit calmer—this is your PAUSE. *This is what worked for you.*

PAUSE may look different each time, and it can be similar each time. Some parents find they consistently use encouraging self-talk. Others find at times it can be staying quiet and next to their child, while other times it is walking away for a moment and focusing on a quick task. There are many ways we PAUSE throughout our days. Paying attention to where we feel pretty darn good *despite* conflict and challenge will help us identify what works best for us.

Once you've discovered what has worked for you to PAUSE, consider other situations in which your way of pausing has shown up. Think about:

Where else has this technique stepped up for you? Where else do you realize you've talked to yourself in encouraging ways, walked away for a moment, taken a deep breath...?

Maybe the answers have nothing to do with parenting at first—and that is okay. What we focus on grows[1], so no matter where you notice your ability to PAUSE, it counts...hugely. Find it and focus on it—even if the only place you can currently PAUSE is while driving in the morning rush hour. Eventually, with practice, you will be able to take it into other situations, and it will become a part of all you do. Now take time to consider this next question:

What was different as a result? How did your PAUSE and ability to be a bit calmer influence the situation, your child, the outcome?

As you consider these questions, use the following journaling space to write down your reflections, what you've noticed, what thoughts and ideas come up for you.

———⌾———

What I'm noticing when I PAUSE...

———⌾———

Taking the time to reflect on what was different as a result of pausing is essential, for it encourages us to keep exercising this muscle. Many parents experience real *Ahas* as they intentionally consider how their PAUSE influenced a situation—clearly connecting how they decided to behave (more calmly!) to how their child did better, things spiraled up less intensely, or what seemed a real problem became a nonissue and no big deal. We can be and feel encouraged, for we can actually *see* how PAUSE is working for us, how it has us feeling better and our children doing better. Isn't this what we all want more of? And the best part is—now we are more likely going to take PAUSE with us into the next challenge or conflict with our child…and *use* it.

Sometimes what is different as a result of us pausing is very small. Maybe *we* feel just a little less stressed and more even-keeled, despite our child still being a total wreck. Perhaps the conflict was still incredibly heated but ended up resolving itself a bit more quickly than usual. No matter how little the difference, it is important to look for it, for the more we pay attention to what it is we want, the more likely it can happen—*what we focus on grows*. The more we exercise our pause muscle, the stronger it becomes.

Ways to PAUSE

Here is a list of ways to PAUSE. I have collected these ideas from parents I've worked with, colleagues, family, and friends, as well as from my own experiences:

- Take several deep breaths
- Count to ten (or a hundred?!)
- Focus on a task
- Say: "I hear you. I need to think about it and I will get back to you."
- Reposition yourself behind a piece of furniture—one father found moving to the opposite side of the kitchen counter was all he needed!
- Break eye contact

- Draw a pause button on your hand or write the word down to visually remind you
- Use encouraging self-talk—"I can do this...This, too, shall pass...He's only four...Breathe, breathe, breathe!"
- Be quiet for a minute or more
- Do something active and brief (for me it was swiping at the kitchen counter)
- Sit next to your child
- Help yourself to a drink of water
- Close your eyes briefly
- Move *slowly* toward your child
- Walk away to another room (maybe to do something like switch a load of laundry or start another task

Take some time and consider what could work for you from this list, what you'd like to begin doing, and what you already do to take that moment to cool off a bit and think. Just writing down a reminder for yourself and putting it where you'll see it often can be enough to let PAUSE step up when losing your temper seems imminent.

Discover, as you keep your attention on pausing, what ways to PAUSE step up the most for you. Reflect on those times when your buttons were pressed and the outcome was chaos, and consider (visualize!) where and how a PAUSE of yours (maybe more than one...) could have made the most difference. Talk about strengthening your pause muscle! Those times when you felt at a total loss and things went from bad to worse can actually be used to help you get better and better at pausing—a do-over of sorts! Truly a gift in disguise.

PAUSE Successes to Encourage You!

Here's a story of a mom I worked with, her three preschool-to elementary-aged children, and red Kool-Aid. You can imagine where this goes! The kids worked hard at helping themselves and pouring and carrying their very RED drinks from counter to table. And yes, they spilled! All over the floor and onto the carpet...yikes. Mom found herself pausing by sticking out her tongue and shaking her head, making a great big "BLLLLLP" sound as her tongue waggled back and forth ☺. She had shared with me previously how she felt a PAUSE for her would have to be getting her adrenaline out—and boy, did she! She now felt a bit better, calmer, and more in control of herself—if not the red Kool-Aid! The funny thing? Her "BLLLLLP" caused her kids to stop dead in their tracks. Mom took full advantage of their PAUSE and calmly, with a light sense of humor, engaged them in cleaning it all up. She was so proud of herself for not losing it! And her kids? They learned a bit more about what it takes to carry full cups of juice, about how to clean spills up (sponges really can be fun to squeeze...), that Mom could be counted on to help them through messes like these, and that there was no need to cry (or scream) over spilt Kool-Aid ☺. What a way to communicate confidence in her kids' ability to learn!

***

Then there is the dad whose twelve-year-old son accidently broke a window in his bedroom. Oops. Glass was everywhere, and it was going to cost plenty to fix it. Before he lost his temper with his son (because...well...it was a mess!), the dad left his son's room and headed downstairs to the garage. There he gathered up the Shop-Vac, some rags, a broom, duct tape, cardboard, and other cleanup and temporary repair items. As he lugged it all up the stairs, he discovered how much calmer he already felt—this PAUSE of leaving the scene of the mess and focusing on what he needed to gather worked for him. He returned to his son's room and engaged him positively in the cleanup. His son, who initially was afraid Dad was going to lose it, was relieved and now receptive and eager to help with the job. And because of Dad's PAUSE, the wonderful learning and connection continued into the next day as they headed to the hardware store together to get all that was necessary for replacing the broken window. The son learned that Dad COULD be counted on to keep it together, that these things were what you needed to use to clean up broken glass, that you could use cardboard and duct tape creatively, and that this is what it takes to replace the window. Perhaps most importantly, he learned that Dad saw him as a capable and competent soul able to take responsibility for the choices (and results!) he made. Awesome.

***

Another parent I know works with adolescents as an aide in a very full and busy classroom. She shared a wonderful PAUSE story with me. She was encouraging a very upset young man to return his focus to the hard work he was doing. His anger and frustration escalated—something he'd had previous challenges with—scaring this aide a bit, which she knew was her "red flag" to PAUSE. She did so by staying quiet for a moment, knowing this could deintensify the situation. Then she reflected on what this student most needed (a chance to cool off). She continued her quiet, giving him the moment to be upset. She began speaking softly to this upset young man. "You know, I need a change of scenery. Would you like to join me on a walk? I'd like your company." Surprised that he said yes, off the two went. She shared with me her next PAUSE—she intentionally stayed silent on their walk, because she felt he needed more space to get control of himself. What respect was communicated! She walked alongside him without trying to make him feel any differently—just gave his upset an okay place to sort itself out. On they went through the halls. Her silence allowed her to tune in to this young man's energy—she could tell when he was calmer, and she began a light conversation with him. By the time they returned to the classroom, he was ready to continue with his work. What did her PAUSE and following calm connection communicate? That she had confidence in this young man's ability to manage himself, and he could count on her as the support *he needed. It also allowed him to have the opportunity to be a bit more successful as a student. Truly empowering!*

***

And a wonderful PAUSE story shared by a parent who follows my business Facebook page: "Live Report from our household: I already wrote 'PAUSE' on my hand after reading your post on pausing, Alice. This morning, my five-year-old wanted to use the iPad (which he hadn't used in months). When I told him in a kind voice, 'Not right now, let's have breakfast first and then play outside,' he gave me a huge temper tantrum with tears and yelling, including calling me a mean word. I paused and let him stomp to his room. He paused for a moment too, but then he threw out a book and slammed the door. I sighed (silently) and paused some more. Then I picked up the book and walked into the room. I paused and looked at my son as kindly as I could before I said, 'You know, books are for reading, not for throwing.' He answered in a whiny-angry voice that he wanted the iPad. I paused again before I answered. 'It makes me sad when you call me names. Right now, your sister and I are having breakfast, and we'd like you to join us.' I gave him a hug and added, 'I understand how you feel.' He pulled away a little. I sat next to my son for a while, and then I walked out. He is still mad at me for not allowing him to have the iPad. I am still in PAUSE mode. It is tough not to react angry and upset about his name-calling and carrying on. I hope we can have a nice rest of the day, hopefully outside. Whew! Goooood Mooooorning! Pause, pause, PAUSE… having another coffee."

What a fantastic story—one that emphasizes how we often just have to keep on pressing our pause button as incidents pile up. Here is how I responded to this parent:

"Fantastic! Your pausing has allowed you to really focus on relationship-building interactions—which, by the way, doesn't mean it is always pretty. What I notice is how your PAUSE of staying quiet for a moment with each exchange not only gave YOU *the opportunity to be intentional with how you responded to him, but also gave your son the opportunity to reflect and think about what he likes and doesn't like, what he can and cannot do. Appreciate yourself right now! I encourage* YOU *to have a 'nice rest of the day' no matter what he decides. Keep me posted on how your day goes!"*

And she did!

"Still sipping my coffee here at the breakfast table. My son decided to join us and is now happily playing with his toy fire truck. Thanks again. We are heading out soon…making a good day 'for myself' (and likely for the kids too)."

THIS is the power of PAUSE and parenting with calm connection.

***

It's all about tipping the balance. I know what you might be thinking right now—probably something along the lines of, "This is so *hard*. I keep forgetting to PAUSE and things keep falling apart. What can I do to get better at this???"

Know that it *is* very difficult to create a PAUSE and calm ourselves as the frustration and anger climb. It took months and months before I'd stopped letting my mad lead the way so often with my teen. Another colleague of mine shared that the process of getting stronger at pausing took several years before she felt calm connection had become her norm. It takes intention and hard work to PAUSE instead of react. And even one success on your part can encourage you to keep on trying, for these successes? They feel so, so much better.

The key here is to **tip the balance** toward calm connection rather than try to be successful all the time only to give up because you forgot, once again, to PAUSE. It is important to give yourself grace—to show yourself compassion, encouragement, forgiveness—and to know that those times you wish you had done it differently are really gifts. Use them for role-modeling for your children what a healthy adult does when mistakes happen: authentically apologize, forgive, be honest about wanting to do things better, persevere and try again. What a way to show our children that we, too, are continuing to do the hard work of growing—of becoming better and better. What a way to show children how to be kind and compassionate, when we can be that way for ourselves.

What can help you tip the balance toward pausing and having calm connection become the norm for you? *Self-care.*[2]

Taking Care of You...

Self-care. I know it is almost crazy to even suggest this—honestly, where is the time? Who has the hours to exercise, be creative, focus on a hobby, or do ANYTHING just for ourselves? Yet caring for ourselves is the foundation for parenting (and living!) well.

I'm sure you already know the difference you feel when you've had a good night's sleep, or a breath of fresh air, or when a friend calls you just when you need her voice the most. This difference? It is the key to the resilience and patience necessary to PAUSE. It is the key for keeping a sense of humor, for being able to be present and tuned in to your child, to have the clarity and confidence in all that you do. *It is essential.* I like to look at self-care as a savings account. **Anything we do, intentionally and just for ourselves, becomes a deposit.** These deposits add up and create the savings account from which we can withdraw in times of challenge and stress. The cool thing? Self-care counts no matter how brief it is. As I wrote in *Parenting Inspired*, even taking a minute just for yourself counts. And a minute we have. Really!

Here are some ideas for self-care gathered from my years of coaching, parenting, and just trying to live well. These may help you start depositing today:

- Making a cup of tea or coffee (drinking it can be a bonus!)
- Spending a moment with a pet
- Sitting down and closing your eyes for a minute
- Gazing out the window or at a favorite photo or piece of art
- Stepping outside to breathe deeply
- Exercising briefly—doing a few yoga stretches, taking a quick, brisk walk around your yard or to the mailbox and back
- Exercising at length—joining a gym, training for a race, walking your dog each day
- Watching a funny YouTube video
- Reading a short article
- Moving forward on a project
- Standing an extra minute in a hot shower
- Turning off or covering your computer screen as you enjoy lunch at your desk
- Calling or texting a friend
- Going out on a date with your partner
- Joining a moms' or dads' group—online or in person
- Sitting quietly in the car before heading into the house after work
- Tinkering in the garage or project room

Try something right now, intentionally and just for you, and notice how it feels. Try something each day—the key is not how long you do something, but that you do it intentionally as something just for you. These deposits truly add up!

Self-care and pausing can be one and the same—*two for the price of one!* I remember two different parents who, during a car ride home with fighting kids in the backseat, chose to pull their car over and step out. This moment gave them the PAUSE they both needed to breathe, get calm, stretch, and NOT listen to the fighting! They truly made a deposit into their self-care accounts, for they were focused on just this—*taking care of themselves*. One of the parents shared her embarrassment over another driver pulling over to make sure all was okay (those screams of fighting kids were heard loud and clear!)—and her ability, despite feeling terribly uncomfortable, to honestly say, "All is okay. I'm taking the break I need…" Upon reentering their cars, even though the yelling continued, these parents had the resilience to drive home without losing it themselves. Their kids? Oh, the fighting and scrabbling went on, but with little to no attention from Mom or Dad, it lost its energy…and by the time both of these parents returned home, things had calmed down, and kids and parents could move into the house and continue on with their day without things spiraling up even more.

I remember the parent who felt like she paused for several years during a tough time with her teen-aged son. Drugs, technology addiction, breaking the law…it all happened. Her PAUSE? Biting her tongue often, seeking her husband's encouragement, calling her friends, taking herself on walks—all of which allowed her time to get clearer on just what she wanted to do for and say to her son. She focused on being clear about a few boundaries for him—ones she knew she could enforce. She focused on connecting with him positively despite how he chose to behave. She worked extremely hard to step out of reacting and step into responding. She didn't have all (at times NONE) of the answers, but she did have—because of her pausing, which had also become regular self-care deposits—the ability to control herself. It took several bumpy, challenging, sometimes downright scary years, but the result? A son who began, on his own, to make better choices, to take school seriously, to say to his parents one day during a family get-together, "You know? Family is the most important thing…"

I remember the mom whose well-meaning husband yet again interrupted the work she was doing to try and have her do it in what he considered a better way. As she was about to bite his head off, she instead took herself into another room and sat, rocking back and forth, in their rocking chair. It felt nice and soothing to her, it helped her calm—truly a deposit into her self-care account as well as a PAUSE. Ten minutes later her husband stepped into the room and said, "I apologize..." Authentically, softly. They both felt immensely better—and connected in a quiet, nice way. This mom shared with me how it was easier for her to practice pausing with her husband than with her kids. She discovered that by focusing on where PAUSE worked for her, she felt more confident in *remembering* to PAUSE and eventually found herself using it as she navigated the chaos of all things children.

Then there was the dad who found his PAUSE to be actively doing something with his hands—he turned to building projects, knitting, even raking, to create the space he needed to feel calmer, and to just plain feel good. He enjoyed projects around the house; he liked to knit simple hats for his kids; and raking—well, he discovered how good it felt to make his yard tidier. I loved how his ways to PAUSE were direct deposits into his Self-Care Savings Account! I think his wife appreciated them, too ☺. The cool thing is, he role-modeled for his elementary and teenaged kids truly productive ways to care for yourself, as well as the importance of hands-on projects and accomplishments. What a difference he made for himself and his family as he grew his ability to focus first on himself with a PAUSE and a self-care deposit. Calm connection slowly began to be the norm, and his relationships with his children got stronger and healthier. Fabulous.

What we focus on grows. I encourage you to use the next journaling space to jot down ways you have deposited into your Self-Care Savings Account, as well as ways you intend to start depositing ☺. Make a note on when this self-care has done double-duty as a PAUSE. Celebrate your effort at strengthening your pause muscle!

———∞∞∞———

I PAUSED! And I took care of me by...

———∞∞∞———

One more note before you move on...we will never completely avoid having our buttons pushed. We will get angry. We will be frustrated and upset. This is totally normal—it is what we do with these feelings that can make all the difference in the world. And this is something we *can* control.

PAUSE is way less about trying to make our child behave and much, much more about focusing first on ourselves, calming ourselves down, and then *responding* instead of reacting.[3] Now we are more likely going to influence our children in positive and productive ways—helping them to take control of their own choices and behavior. It is about tipping the balance toward regularly exercising our pause muscle and growing our ability to respond with calm connection leading the way.

Notice and appreciate your red flags, discover what works for you to PAUSE, remember (often!) how it feels and what is different when you use PAUSE successfully (what we focus on grows…). Deposit regularly into your Self-Care Savings Account, and watch your life change. For it will—from less intense conflict to children who listen and learn, to a connection with your child that feels strong and good, to discovering the power of parenting and living with calm connection in all you do.

Getting Your MAD Out!

Maybe as you've been reading up to this point, you have been nodding your head, agreeing, able to visualize and understand the power of PAUSE and how it can really support you in parenting well and connecting with your children in truly relationship-building ways—or just simply helping things spiral up less and leaving you a bit less frazzled ☺. But you also may be thinking that sometimes, just sometimes, you really don't want to be calm—*you just want to be mad.*

Here's the deal. Becoming intentional about all you do is an important result of exercising your pause muscle and (in time) taking it deeper. That space that initially is used for calming yourself down in order to respond rather than react during a heated moment? It has you becoming clearer and more mindful and intentional in all you do. **Including choosing to be mad.**

As one parent said to me, "Sometimes I choose to *not* PAUSE and just BE mad." Yes—*choosing* to be mad. Here's the really cool thing—this parent? She actually has taken PAUSE deeper. She has just expressed one of the gifts internalizing PAUSE brings us—to be intentional in *all* we do. I pointed this out to her—that she *chooses* to "just get her mad out." Intentionally. With purpose. *In control of her choices.* Instead of flying off the handle and reacting to something, she has made an intentional decision to just be mad. It felt reassuring to her as she realized that by choosing to intentionally get her mad out, she was actually pausing…and becoming more able to role-model for her children healthy ways to be mad.

Throughout this book you will learn how to grow your ability to be in control of yourself, to be calm and connected with your kids, yourself, and others. To let the power of parenting with calm connection weave its way into all parts of your life. It is equally important to know that this doesn't mean we, too, don't have big feelings or upset moments...that we don't feel deeply sad or mad or anxious. We are supposed to—we are human. It is what we *do* with our feelings that matters.

Sometimes we just aren't going to be calm...but we *can* be in control. PAUSE allows us to focus on ourselves, first and foremost—to decide what we want and how we are going to present it. And sometimes what we want is to be mad. I know when I've decided to just BE mad as my daughter or spouse pushes my button, my mad "looks" different. It is expressed in ways like this: "That makes me so MAD. I really don't like it. I mean it when I say NO..." It is spoken from a place of intention and clarity, allowing my feelings to be heard and maybe even understood. That is what makes it different from fly-off-the-handle mad—it can be more likely heard and understood.

Think about this—PAUSE and finding a place of calm and then stepping in to respond instead of react is always the goal; it is always to be at the forefront of your actions. PAUSE is a muscle we need to exercise and get stronger, so that in time, we've tipped the balance toward truly healthy relating. But I think it can be equally valuable to PAUSE and then intentionally be upset. I think it is essential, for it shows our children that all of our feelings matter and can be expressed from that in-control place that internalizing PAUSE gives us. What a way to role model healthy expression. I know from my own intentional decisions to not PAUSE (or so I thought, for just thinking this has created one!), some rather hot and uncomfortable exchanges have unfolded. And there's the key—they've "unfolded." They've been expressed and shared, and ultimately, all those involved part ways (another PAUSE!) feeling—at the least—heard. And then we've come back together calm(er), clear(er), more able to collaborate. A healthy discussion (eventually) follows. And now our relationship just got a bit stronger. A hotly contested issue turns into a more positive collaboration. What a relationship-building skill—to be able to take a hotly contested anything and emerge with some kind of healthy collaboration. This, from still choosing to be mad.

I encourage you to notice what is different for you when you are upset and you tell yourself, "I'm just going to go ahead and BE mad!" Recognize you've actually just paused…and it is okay to still be upset. Really. As you work on strengthening your pause muscle, look for the times you've still expressed ALL your feelings AND ended up with a healthy discussion and (eventual) collaboration. Those times are there, and they are relationship building. Truly!

This may be where you want to PAUSE in this book and stay focused on the basics—a "time out" of sorts, so you can think and practice and rest. Small steps—such as doing something for just a minute each day that's just for you, or intentionally noticing when you do feel calmer or more connected—can be enough. Small steps are easier to stick with, and when we continue to take them over time, real and positive change can occur. So PAUSE right now. Breathe. And sit in the basics of pausing. You'll know if and when you are ready to move on and take PAUSE deeper. Either way, you are making a real difference for the ones you love the most.

**PAUSE and the power of calm
connection transforms relationships…
bringing greater ease, confidence and
joy to your parenting.**

Taking PAUSE Deeper

Can you imagine what it could be like to use PAUSE and the power of calm connection in all that you do? To really experience it weaving its way all through your day, with all of your relationships? Imagine...

Let's Start with a Story:

"Here we go again..." Tina, already dragging from a frustrating day at the office, sighed to herself as her twelve-year-old step-daughter, Katie, proceeded with The Silent Treatment on their way home from school—complete with The Eye Roll and crossing her arms as she stared out the window. All Tina had done was say, "Tell me about your day!" with the hope of hearing something that could take her mind off of her especially trying afternoon with less-than-cooperative employees. The next fifteen minutes of their drive home was spent in silence. Tina began to fume inside herself, wondering just WHAT it would take to get this child to show her some respect and ANSWER her. Biting her tongue and choosing to stay quiet gave Tina the PAUSE she knew she needed so she and Katie wouldn't end up in a yelling match in the car. And it gave Tina the time to think about just what needed to happen once they were home to hopefully keep things under control (herself included ☺).

The car door slammed as Katie continued The Silent Treatment, stomping off to her bedroom. "Man," thought Tina. "What is up with that child?" She threw together a much-needed snack for both of them and followed Katie up to her room, stopping to knock first. Poking her head in, she asked if she could join her. Silence filled the room, but with no other signs of resistance, Tina joined Katie and sat next to her, offering the snack she'd brought. Tina continued her PAUSE by just staying put and refusing to let the view of dirty laundry strewn all over the floor, school work in disarray, or even the leftover dishes from yesterday's snack get under her skin. "Nope," she thought to herself, "now's not the time to remind her of the rules in our house."

After a few minutes of quiet companionship, out it poured: "I HATE school! The girls are so MEAN. I never want to go back!"

"Whew...It sounds like a bad day," Tina responded. Then she lay down next to Katie, rubbing her back and letting her finish her cry. It wasn't long until Katie sat back up, and together, she and Tina talked about her day, how she felt, what she could do right now to feel better. What could have been an escalating disaster turned into a relationship-building experience for Katie and Tina. Tina was relieved. It had been a long and bumpy road getting to this place of connection that exercising her pause muscle had created. But now it was paying off. She felt pretty darn good about how their relationship was coming along. She found she felt a bit better overall—even with work stresses hanging over her head and dinner and chores and paperwork to be done tonight.

But the calm didn't last. Later, while Tina and Katie waded through homework during a haphazard dinner Tina threw together, trouble began. Katie's Dad, Mike, came home, tired and grumpy from a long day at work and irritated to be greeted by what felt like even more craziness at home. Katie, already on edge due to all her homework, stomped off to her room to avoid her dad's bad mood. Though the timing was questionable with Mike already feeling irritated and grumpy,

Tina went ahead and shared with him The Silent Treatment and all that had followed. True to form, Mike only heard the initial yuck and exploded, "When will she ever learn to be respectful to you? I'm going to give her something to chew on..." Tina just barely caught him before he stormed in to give Katie a piece of his mind. She really didn't want to rock that boat, as she and Katie had reached a tenuous truce over snacks and a good cry. Mike and Tina argued about how to (or whether he even should!) approach Katie. Katie reappeared and joined in with, "DAD! You just don't GET it. I HATE you!" Round and round they went, yelling and pleading with each other until, exhausted, they headed off in opposite directions ignoring each other. Tina was at her wits end. It had been a strenuous day overall; it had taken all she had to deal with The Silent Treatment. The calm connection, she knew, had made a real difference for her and Katie. But now the kitchen looked like a war zone, and she and Mike were knocking heads, while Katie and her dad were in a real battle! This was not how she wanted family life to be.

Sound familiar? You've worked at pausing and being calm with your child, and it IS feeling better…but you still feel overwhelmed. Life is still chaotic. Other relationships in the mix are struggling. Tina (in our story) is in that place. I've been there, too. **But it doesn't have to be this way.** The more we can strengthen ourselves using PAUSE and the calm connection that can follow, the more the rest of the chaos (especially within ourselves as we struggle), calms down.

I was right where Tina was as I began to strengthen my pause muscle. I was getting it together with my teen, feeling better about the way she and I related, feeling more confident in listening to her and being with her as she shared her upset. It took a lot of work, calming my anxiety as she shared the hurt and pain she was feeling. It took a lot of work to PAUSE, quiet the churning within me (though rarely getting rid of it), and allow her to fully express her (at times) over-the-top ideas. I so wanted to say NO before she even got her words out of her mouth. You see, dealing with *my* feelings of anxiety over *her* ideas was often overwhelming, and NO seemed to be the only way out. But like Tina, PAUSE was exercised, anxiety tamped down at least a bit, and calm connection began to be more of our norm. Surprisingly, some of those moments listening to seemingly crazy ideas or watching definitely crazy antics actually became the coolest experiences of all—because I paused. Like the time she got stuck on a mountain with a friend—stuck enough that they required help from others and were hours late getting home. Their crazy idea to climb up into unfamiliar territory, unbeknownst to their hiking group, left them truly scared. Having to be talked down a mountain one step at a time by the hiking buddies who had found them left the girls feeling surprisingly vulnerable—a rarely admitted feeling from a teen, and surprising, because these were girls who had grown up on mountains and knew the risks and rules of back-country exploring. It was scary for us at home—wondering why our daughter was so late, knowing she had gone hiking in the mountains, not having any cell-phone coverage to check in with, wondering if she was okay.

Why did this become one of the coolest experiences? Because we all grew in truly healthy ways that day. My teen discovered a more courageous self. She accepted her responsibility in the choices she had made and the results that followed. She understood the danger and appreciated the help. She openly shared her experience with her dad and me. She found productive ways to process her upset over it all—she and her friend designed a T-shirt depicting an honest yet humorous take on their experience, and she wrote an apology to the father who was with the group of teens on this hike. My husband and I, despite our intense anxiety, exercised our pause muscles by staying quiet as she opened up to us. I want to emphasize how incredibly tough this PAUSE was for us as we heard the description of actions that made no sense, that seemed crazy from the outset. Yet our PAUSE allowed us to listen to her instead of criticizing her judgment. We asked questions rather than dictated the "You should have…" We got stronger in our ability to PAUSE and connect in a respectful, positive way, and our daughter got stronger inside of herself. She became more aware of her limits and abilities, of what feels good to her and what doesn't, and of how to listen to and trust her intuition. Our relationship got stronger too—she felt she could come to us as the resource we intended to be. She *wanted* to share even her scariest feelings and craziest ideas with us. She began to ask for and accept *our* thoughts and ideas. She began to believe and listen to us when we said, "Be prepared!" Now THAT was totally awesome.

Like Tina, I was feeling truly connected to my daughter, and it felt wonderful. It highlighted for me how much I wanted this feeling in all areas of my life...and how it wasn't always there. I wanted this feeling with both my girls, with my husband, with my friends, in my work, on the road, at the grocery store. I wanted to feel connected and wonderful a whole lot more. I wanted more JOY.

**Let calm connection lead the
way in all you do and discover the
gentle joy that can follow...**

The Power of Living with Calm Connection

Imagine what it would be like to live PAUSE. To let it calm everything down inside you as you lead with calm connection in all that you do. To discover greater clarity on what you want in a situation, with your children, in a conflict or challenge. To discover greater confidence in yourself, a deeper awareness and acceptance of feelings—both yours and others'. To find yourself becoming way more intentional in all you do—mindful, present, purposeful. To experience greater ease in being in uncomfortable situations and feelings. **To be the calm, confident, positive influence your child needs the most**. The calm, confident person you WANT to be. Taking PAUSE deeper means living it as your norm. Think of PAUSE at its basic like a switch you turn on and off in those button-pushing moments. Over time, the pause muscle strengthens so much that you begin to live from a place of calm connection in ALL you do. This is taking PAUSE deeper. **Imagine** knowing without a doubt that you can move through whatever chaos is presented to you and feel balanced, calm, and clear in just what you need to do. Think about how you can now influence the chaos, others, the outcome in uplifting and affirming ways.

Imagine...having the clarity of knowing just what you want and need to do in any situation you are in—challenges, everyday experiences, conflicts—and trusting fully in how you decide to respond. This kind of clarity? It is less about knowing exactly what you are going to say or do, and way more about trusting your response because it is based on what feels right and good from inside you.

It is the kind of clarity that has you focused on how you'd like things to be—for instance, the kind of adults you hope your children will become or the qualities you want to encourage in them or how you hope your relationship with them will be. On a simpler level, it's the clarity to know how you'd like the family vacation to go, or how you'd like to feel by the end of your day. This clarity of your "end in mind"[1] has you responding in the moment based on what you really want. I was introduced to this "end in mind" idea in *7 Habits of Highly Effective Families* by Stephen Covey and in *ScreamFree Parenting*; I also shared it with you in *Parenting Inspired*. This concept allows you to act in alignment with the "end" you have in mind, rather than to react to all the emotions or circumstances of the moment. Let me give you a simple and probably familiar example.

Back when my girls were little and I had errands to run, I knew without a doubt that I wanted to be home in time for them to nap in their own beds (which meant a more peaceful afternoon and easier evening, with solid sleep tucked under their belts). I knew, without a doubt, I wanted my girls *ready and willing* for naps in their own beds—which meant I might get a much needed nap as well, or time to accomplish something else I wanted or needed to do. With this end in mind, I intentionally chose to do fewer errands so I could be calm and present enough to make it a good experience for my girls—including them in the process of shopping, giving them time to ask questions or find what we needed "all by themselves." I could patiently let them count (and maybe recount) the five apples we wanted or find the exact loaf of bread that was their favorite. With a clear goal of getting home on time and in good spirits, I knew that I had to minimize errands and draw upon my patience (necessary when shopping with young children!). This usually got me the result I wanted—naps for all and a more enjoyable evening. Being clear on where you intend to head and what you intend to grow can be essential for parenting and living well—whether it is naps in your own bed (!) or kind, respectful, self-directed children and future adults.

*Imagine...*feeling truly confident in yourself—the kind of confidence that has you stepping into the often scary unknown (as I did with my teen on that mountain) and being able to embrace where it takes you—to trust fully that it is exactly where you need to be in order to learn and grow the most. This kind of confidence? It is quietly certain rather than loudly defended. It is about feeling curious rather than critical. Think about what could be different with the scary unknown if you were to feel quietly certain that you *could* step into it and do it well...that no matter what, *you will be okay.* Now you can actually be open and receptive to that scary unknown and more likely to move through it productively, even if it feels difficult or unnerving.

*Imagine...*being comfortable (or nearly so ☺) in ALL your child's feelings *and* yours—no matter how deep, loud, over-the-top, exciting, confusing, delightful, or concerning they are. Consider the benefit to your child—or anyone—when they know, without a doubt, their feelings can be expressed safely with you. Imagine how it could be for *you*, whether you were totally down in the dumps or over-the-top anxious, to actually accept and sit in your feelings rather than trying desperately to make them go away. Sit, affirm, accept...and discover the gentle compassion you can give yourself and how you can feel a bit more empowered and able to move through these difficult times. Imagine a deeper awareness of and acceptance for ALL feelings— whether your child's, a friend's, your spouse's, or your own. What a way to grow ourselves as the whole and wonderful beings we are, ultimately enriching our lives in deeply meaningful ways.

*Imagine...*becoming more intentional about what you do and how you do things; being present and mindful no matter where you are or the chaos you are in; having a focus that allows you to really listen, communicate clearly, stay quiet when needed, and communicate respect for and confidence in another. Think about how this intentional presence allows you to move with a quiet gentleness through your day. Quiet, because you are present and listening with greater care to your children, to yourself, to others; gentle, because you find you move with quiet certainty and purpose, slowing down and softening your approach—perhaps reaching more gently toward your child, using a softer voice, adding the twinkle in your eye that can lighten a difficult moment. Consider how your children, your partner, your friends now feel as you listen more, talk less, and walk alongside them in this gentler manner.

*Imagine...*knowing you are the calm, confident, positive leader your child needs in order to grow well—no matter how they are currently behaving or what their choices are or what big feelings they are showing. Knowing, *without a doubt*, your influence is guiding them well and you are truly trusting *their* journey as they learn and grow. Imagine this kind of trust. Trust in yourself, and in the process of growth; trust that every situation is one that you can learn from and one that will help you grow a bit more toward your best self...your child toward their best self; TRUST in pausing and allowing the power of calm connection to lead you through life, knowing you are always heading in the best direction for you; TRUST from the inside out, filled with quiet confidence in all you do.

PAUSE is the key to living your life with clarity, calm, and the deeper connection that grows your relationships in healthy, positive, lovely, and meaningful ways.

———⋘———

Imagine knowing...

**That all you really need to do is
PAUSE and focus first on yourself in order to
be the calm, confident, positive influence
you and your children need the most.**

**To live and parent with calm
connection in all you do.**

———⋘———

Now what could be different for you? I believe your life can change—certainly your relationships can—in wonderfully lifting, more deeply meaningful, definitely satisfying, and ultimately joyful ways. **Imagine.**

PAUSE for a Better, more Peaceful Life

Let's stop imagining and get busy helping you take PAUSE deeper in order to bring greater satisfaction and more joy to your life, your relationships, to all that you do. Let PAUSE—and the power of calm connection you are finding as you parent—guide you in all aspects of your life, from parenting to living. **Let what you imagine become what you live.**

What *can* you do to harness the power of PAUSE and calm connection and let it change your life? How can you strengthen and continue to grow what you are doing with your children and have it weave itself into *all* that you do, with *all* of your relationships? Let's begin with some things I like to explore with my clients, myself, and anyone working toward the power of parenting AND living with calm connection. Take your time to read and process these questions and use the spaces available for jotting down your thoughts and ideas:

1. *Think about when you have truly felt at your BEST.* [2]

Consider what being at your best means to you; consider when and where you've felt this way over the years—with your parenting, or with any other aspect of your life, whatever comes to mind. You know when you've been at your best—it was those times that felt so right and good…you were confident and clear, content in what you were doing and whom you were with. When I think of when I've felt the best ME, I immediately think about all the times I spent immersed in all things toddler. The memories (and current opportunities!) of toddler adventures I've had always put a smile on my face—from the long walk that took us no further than the end of the block (what with all the worms, rocks, and puddles to study or play in, and the airplanes to crank our heads up and watch 'til they disappeared, who could possibly walk any further?!), to the falling-apart alligator tears and me feeling completely comfortable and welcoming no matter the toddler feelings OR antics. I have always been at my best with toddlers—truly content, relaxed, delighting in my time with them, confident in all that I do as I guide them.

A colleague of mine gave an example of being at her BEST when coaching a parent through tough times with her young teen. She felt totally present and focused, open and curious. Her conversation with her client flowed, they both felt connected and at ease—even as they talked through difficult things together and made some tough choices. Her client felt safe enough to cry, laugh, and share honestly and openly. My colleague found she was clear on the questions to ask and the areas to explore, successfully guiding the parent toward creating the kinds of positive change the parent wanted the most for herself and her teen. My colleague was confident she left her client feeling supported and encouraged, and *she* was energized by the entire coaching session. I remember how she told me it left her smiling all day long!

A parent I coached shared with me that he felt his BEST self when he was immersed in a project at work. He was clear on what the project goals were, and he felt energetic and focused. He enjoyed his team of coworkers—working creatively and productively together. He talked of how, even though the project was difficult and time-consuming and stretched deadlines, he was at ease rather than stressed. He shared the positive energy that defined this experience...the satisfaction he felt about doing his job well and feeling confident in his work.

One mother I know reflected on her just-out-of-college days and her decision to leave the place where she had spent all her life and move to Alaska. No job awaited her; she just felt the desire to pack up and leave and land in a new place. Despite the unknown and uncertainty, she recalled how alive she felt—delighting in the travel, excited to meet new people, totally at ease and confident in her ability to find a job and place to live. She remembered this time as one in which she felt at her BEST—and mused over how this adventurous move that had felt so right and good to her (and crazy to *her* parents!) had led her to the job that became a career and to the man she married and the family she then raised.

Take some time and reflect on when you have felt at your BEST. It could have been a time oh-so-long-ago, perhaps while you were still in school. Several parents have shared with me how they really felt their BEST when they were part of a sports team, or studying a subject that really excited them. It could've been just an hour early last week, when you found yourself perusing your favorite cookbook, jotting down new recipes to try, rummaging through your cupboard to see what ingredients you already had, making a solid plan for shopping and cooking. Or maybe it isn't just a past experience. Maybe your BEST time is when you head into the library with your child, confident in how they'll behave and the good time you'll have together. You enjoy discovering and reading new books with your child, and you always find a chance to connect with another adult and enjoy a quiet and quick conversation.

No matter what comes to mind, take a moment to really think about it. Use the space provided to write some of it down.

⸺∞⸺

I was at my *BEST* when...

⸺∞⸺

2. ***Think about what qualities of your "Best Self times" really stand out to you.***

Reflect on the memories that have come to mind of your Best Self. Consider how you were feeling—including what feelings come up right now as you think about these moments. Describe yourself at these times—identify the qualities/feelings that really stand out to you. For me, it was when I was with a toddler—I felt completely present and engaged, observant, gentle and certain in all I did, receptive to whatever the toddler time presented me. I felt complete trust in myself...quietly confident and full of wonder. As I write this and think about these times, I find a smile spreads across my face and my heart warms once again ☺—the bonus of taking time to reflect!

My colleague felt focused, present, and connected. She felt clear on how to support the parent she was working with and energized by their conversation. The father who shared of his work project felt creative and confident in what he was doing, productive and at ease despite a challenging process. The mother who moved to Alaska felt adventurous, trusting (in herself!), curious, and comfortable. Many others speak of feeling centered and confident when at their BEST.

Use the box below to write how you felt at these times, what qualities really stood out, and anything else that describes your Best Self stories:

------ ∞ ------

When I was at my BEST, I felt...

------ ∞ ------

3. ***Now, consider what would happen if these Best Self Qualities were the norm for you—if these stories of who you are at your BEST were your daily experience. What could be different for you? What could be different for your children? For others in your life?***

If I could be present and engaged, gentle in all I did, receptive to whatever was presented to me…If I could have complete trust in myself, be quietly confident and full of wonder, then my time with my daughters and husband—with anyone—would become full of rich and meaningful experiences that we could all find real joy in. My girls would experience a mother who'd listen and ask questions far more than she'd talk and direct. My girls would know without a doubt they could count on me for anything. They would feel heard, understood, encouraged—they would be empowered to live their lives with the kind of love and respect for themselves and others that, to me, is essential. I would delight in all of their ups and downs, knowing for certain ALL parts of their journey are key for growing whole and wonderful human beings. I'd worry no more (okay, less…) and instead trust that they are exactly where they need to be to learn and grow the most. I'd discover what I could do to best support them as they faced struggles, and I'd be able to affirm and encourage and maybe just sit with them and their feelings. Wow. Wouldn't that be awesome? And guess what? I am already being this way and living this life at least some of the time—and I'm slowly tipping the balance toward making it the norm. You can do the same.

What an AHA moment for me when I realized that, despite (or maybe because of?) the turmoil and upset and still trying to PAUSE more often, I actually *was* letting my Best Self Qualities step up more and more. As I let PAUSE give me the space I needed, and as I grew my ability to let calm connection lead the way, I discovered those Best Self stories back in toddler days were now a part of the new stories developing with my teens. I was observing more and talking (a bit!) less. I was finding it easier to be present and stay engaged, even when faced with an eye rolling, "I TOLD you already, Mom" teen. I felt right and good from inside me, no matter what my daughters presented me with.

THIS is what taking PAUSE deeper and the power of calm connection can do for you. PAUSE leads us to be and live our best selves. It gives us the space—mentally, emotionally, and even physically—to become more mindful, intentional, and clear in all we do, allowing us to choose with care how we intend our relationships, our family life, and ourselves to be. It allows us to create more of what we truly want—those healthy, connected, joyful relationships.

Now let's put our attention to ways you can take PAUSE deeper and truly live from a place of calm connection, with your Best Self Qualities stepping to the forefront in all (or at least most!) of what you do. Read through the following practices that I've gathered from personal use, parents I've worked with, colleagues, friends, and family members. Try on the ones that resonate the most. The key is, **what you focus on grows**—so even if you can only put your attention to one of these for short moments at a time, it ALL counts and will help you get stronger. Use the journaling spaces provided for any writing that may help you keep your attention on what you are trying to grow. Let's go!

Practices for Taking PAUSE Deeper

Quiet Time or Meditation—This can range from a minute of sitting quietly before (re)entering the chaos around you, to lengthier times that involve a varied list of practices—including just taking the time to make and hold a hot cup of coffee or tea, journaling perhaps, or reading something short that inspires you. I remember when my girls were little, what worked for me was pausing in my bedroom, sitting on the edge of my bed, and gazing out the window for just a minute. That's all I could do—a minute (sometimes less, as they burst through the door with "Mommy!"). And it was a deposit into what I knew I wanted to grow over time—lengthy quiet, meditation, or prayer time.

Another parent spoke of sitting in her car at daycare pick-up time—using an extra few minutes to sit quietly, regrouping and letting work stress go before heading in to greet her toddler. I also remember when I was a nanny for a toddler and preschooler—after loading them into the car, I'd sit in the front seat and say nothing. After the hammering from them to get going and "What are you doing, Alice???" I'd let them know I was taking a minute to be quiet. It didn't take too many times until I'd find each of them closing their eyes or playing quietly in the backseat as they waited for me to center and calm. One minute. You can do this! And you will discover that a minute can power you through an entire day. An essential thing to remember is this is *not* the time to scroll through your texts, respond to messages, or double-check your grocery list. This is just a time to rest your eyes, breathe, and relax fully—or at least a bit ☺.

Positive Self-Talk—Intentionally take that negative reaction in your head and switch it up to something more affirming, positive, appreciative. From, "Arghhh! He's driving me crazy!" to "Man, he's having a difficult time and I can be patient." From "I'm going to lose it!" to "Breathe, breathe, breathe…this, too, shall pass." From "I just don't know what to do!" to "The solution will come; right now I'm just going to PAUSE…"

One example I can share is what I do on the days I have to drag myself out of bed in the morning after a rough night of little, if any, sleep. Instead of focusing on the exhaustion I feel and how crummy the day might now be, I say, "Boy, that cup of coffee is going to taste s-o-o-o good, and I deserve it!" I find I start to look forward to an excellent cup—and a bit of chocolate to go with it—even as I still toss and turn in bed. As a result, I let go of that exhaustion—instead of having it drag me down, I use it as the reason I get to treat myself. And that has me feeling better, more energized, more accepting of my tired. And my day? It often goes much, much better. Here are some other ways in which you can redirect negative thoughts to positive, more lifting ones:

- "She is so STUBBORN!" to "She sure is clear about what she wants!"
- "If only this traffic would speed up! Urgh…I'm going to be so late to work. I'll never get the project done in time!" to "I intend to drive safely and patiently. I know I'll be late, but I intend to feel good about all I *do* accomplish today."

- "My child is NOT math-oriented at all; it's always a struggle!" to "My child is working hard learning new math skills."
- "My toddler makes a mess out of everything!" to "My toddler is so curious about how everything works—she really is exploring her world!"
- "I am a wreck! How am I ever going to get through this?" to "This is really hard for me, but I know what I can do to move through this well."
- "I can't take this anymore!" to "Patience, patience, breathe, patience…just one more minute. I can do this…"
- "Everyone is falling apart. We are going to have a terrible night!" to "Everyone is falling apart! I am certain we can make tonight easier on all of us…"

The cool thing about switching your self-talk from negative to positive and affirming is how you feel after doing it for a while. You'll notice a bit more energy, hope, and purposefulness. Your thoughts will now be focused on what you really want, and over time, this is powerfully uplifting. At first you'll notice small differences…and as you stay focused on your self-talk and choosing with care what you say, you will discover how, more and more, things seem to go in the direction you think. How cool is that? *Things will go in the direction you think.* So think with care, intention, and appreciation!

Intentional Affirmations—Similar to positive self-talk, this focuses on how you are thinking about yourself or another. It is about noticing and appreciating the qualities, strengths, and feelings involved, no matter the challenge or the ease of a situation. Maybe you lost your temper over something your toddler or teen did. Take the moment and affirm how MAD you felt (and expressed, perhaps too loudly), and appreciate that it comes from a place of deep care and compassion that you have for your child. Tell yourself: "I really lost it. This is really hard for me…I feel so deeply because I care so much." *What a strength that is, to care so deeply.* Taking the moment to affirm and appreciate this creates the PAUSE that can encourage you to step in more calmly and ultimately influence more positively. Here are more examples of Intentional Affirmations:

- "Despite the crazy day, I put a hot meal on the table for dinner—and at least two of us enjoyed it," (as you find yourself initially fretting over the crazy schedule that has your family going in many different directions…).
- "It's easy for me to stay calm and be patient with my friend's child. I know I can get better with my own."
- "Even though bedtime was STILL full of tears and fights, I only yelled twice tonight. I AM getting better at pausing!"
- "Ahhhh…I can tell how creative my kids were today!" (as you gaze at the MESS that has engulfed your house).
- "I'm having trouble looking forward to this event. I wonder what I can do to encourage myself?"
- "I did well today! I kept it together nearly all day long!" (rather than beating yourself up for the stress of the evening and your—and the kids'—eventual meltdowns).
- "There's still a lot to be done, and I feel good about the few things I did do."
- "He remembered to pack his lunch into his backpack!" (as you look around at the homework folder, outdoor gear, and other school necessities spread across the floor).
- "I'm sorry I yelled. I'm exhausted, and it means so much to me to have help with all the chores so we can have family time together."
- "I'm glad I could at least listen to my daughter as she unloaded all those upset feelings. I hope next time I can think of more ways to help her."
- "I worked hard at staying quiet and just listening at first," (following jumping into the middle of your teen's latest struggle a bit too soon and her letting you know loud and clear that you did so!).
- "All my worry and anxiety for my daughter really shows how deeply I love and want the best for her. THIS I can appreciate…"

Take time with the journaling space provided to write a few affirming statements to yourself—erase the "I should, I wish, if I only had..." words that might first show up as you write. Erase them and use "I could, I intend, here's what I DID do..." And notice how it feels as you practice reframing an experience and truly validating yourself. I believe you'll discover a bit of a lift, and that lift can carry you into the next moment with more energy, optimism, and even inspiration.

—⚬⚬⚬—

Here's how I affirmed myself today!

—⚬⚬⚬—

Appreciation—Look to what you CAN appreciate, despite its being really difficult or trying or button-pushing. Better yet, appreciate where it is easy to at first—usually when things are going well and you already feel good. Then look at the more difficult moments. Take time to notice and appreciate where your Best Self Qualities do show up, however briefly. Notice and appreciate wherever, whenever, and whomever you can. Appreciation goes a long way toward helping you grow just what you want more of. Consider creating a "gratitude journal," or simply use the following journaling space to write down all that you notice. Perhaps appreciate:

- The sunshine after a particularly rainy day, or the rain after a particularly dry stretch, even if it means indoor play all day long.
- The uninterrupted four(!) hours of sleep you got…
- The fellow who let you go in front of him in the grocery check-out line—somehow he just knew you and your kids needed to get out as quickly as possible!
- The brief smile your teen gave you right before (or after!) she rolled her eyes.
- How you find it easy to talk openly with your friend (even though you struggle doing so with your partner).
- How your kids getting the flu all at once had you letting go of all those "have-tos" and instead actually enjoying just hanging out with your sick kids—watching favorite movies, reading favorite books, finding new and creative ways to eat buttered toast…☺
- The way you can be depended on to make dinner several times a week.
- Your spouse's "constructive criticism" as an indicator of his or her desire for a better experience…or teamwork…or more family time…or a more relaxed YOU…
- How you think creatively and can really move forward on projects.
- The talent you have at organizing—even if it goes unnoticed or untapped in your own home ☺.
- How deeply you care (which is why your worry is over the top at times).

- The way you DID pause and step in initially with a calm demeanor...even if you then promptly lost it.
- Your toddler's constant NOs, for as frustrating and exhausting as they may be, they are also a sign of his growing independent self—something you really do want more of!
- Your teen's resistance to all things parental, as they're working hard at standing in their conviction—key for that future, self-directed adult.
- Finally climbing into your comfortable and warm bed after the toughest day of all...and having a good cry. Oh, yes. A good, good cry.
- The piles of pillows, stuffed animals, flashlights, and blankets on the living room floor as a sign of the incredible focused and creative play that had your kids engaged all afternoon—instead of the mess that it is.
- The constant whining of your preschooler—it is her way of communicating clearly what she thinks she wants! Clear communication. It really is a good thing.

If appreciating feels like too much of a stretch, I encourage you to make a list of *what puts a smile on your face.* From there, appreciation is just a step away. It often starts with us only being able to find one thing we can appreciate at the end of an overwhelming day. That one thing? It counts. This practice? It is powerful.

I remember one parent I worked with who, when asked what she could appreciate about her daughter (with whom she was really, really struggling), could only come up with one answer—how she slept in her own bed each night. She agreed to focus on what else she could appreciate during the week between our coaching sessions. And the next session? Her list had tripled. The week after that? She had a list so long that she was practically dancing with joy—it felt so wonderful to her to rediscover all the things about her daughter that delighted her. You can imagine how that then influenced their relationship. *What we focus on grows.* There were times when all I could appreciate was the fact that I was still here—standing in the midst of the chaos—that I hadn't thrown in the towel and given up.

PAUSE

—◦◦◦—

I noticed and appreciated...

—◦◦◦—

Presence—This is giving your intentional and full presence to whatever you are doing. When your phone rings and the pot is boiling over and the dog needs to go out NOW and your children are whiny and clingy...presence is "I see you need my attention. I am going to answer my phone and let the dog out, then I can listen to you." And then you turn your attention to what you said you were going to do... and when done, follow through with listening to your (now screaming, perhaps) child. PAUSE gives you the moment to breathe, clarify the priority (Phone? Child? Dog?), and then mindfully step back into the chaos, communicating clearly what it is you intend to do.

Presence. We get caught up in juggling, multi-tasking, trying to work, cook, text, clean, and appease our kids all at once. This habit will never entirely go away, but with your intentional and full presence to each piece of what you are trying to do, you will discover that calm connection begins to weave its way through. You feel calmer. You feel more connected to your child, to the person you are texting, to the delicious meal you are trying to cook. Now, instead of waiting for all of it to STOP so you can feel relieved, relaxed, and finally able to enjoy yourself, you are more relaxed *during* the million things you are now accomplishing one at a time. And enjoying it more often. Really! Just imagine—no longer waiting for something to be done in order to feel good. Instead, feeling good no matter the things still needing to be done!

Reframing and Do-overs—Reframe that tumultuous, upsetting experience you got caught up in earlier by asking yourself what opportunity it gave you or your child, what strengths of yours were called forth, what gifts came as a result—what you could appreciate despite the yuck—or because of the yuck!

Maybe you realize, now that you have a bit of distance from it all and have calmed down, that it was an opportunity for you to discover your limits when it comes to having your button pushed repeatedly. What a way to be that much more aware of your needs as you step into the next round of button-pushing—and maybe do it differently as a result. Or maybe everyone falling apart and ending up in their rooms gave your children the opportunity to discover how a bit of time and space can help tremendously when it comes to feeling and doing better. Or perhaps you realize you really did call upon your patience—at length. It's just that your patience wore out! Maybe you can see how, *because* of all the yuck, you and your child ended up reconnecting with extra big hugs that left a smile lingering in your heart. Those hugs? Truly a gift.

Reframing means looking for the opportunity, gift, or what did work in a challenging situation. This allows you to relax a bit, let go of the guilt over losing your temper or behaving poorly, and feel a bit more compassionate with yourself and more connected to your child. For me, reframing lets me melt away the roadblock I feel due to my frustration or anger. I find I "soften" physically as I allow my reframing to lead me to appreciating…which leads me to the calm connection I intend to live by.

Or you can think it through with a "do-over" in mind, thinking about where you could have paused, what could have been different if calm connection had led the way, if your Best Self Qualities had permeated the entire situation. Think about what it might have required from you—what strengths would need to be called upon (patience...resilience...humor...?). And most importantly, think about what might have been different for your children and for the outcome of the situation if your do-over was the reality. What we focus on grows, so reframing, thinking through a do-over, and always, always appreciating something within it all, are key for tipping the balance toward parenting with calm connection as your norm.

What we focus on grows—You've read these words often in this book because they are essential for creating the positive change you want the most. They are also another practice for growing your pause muscle and the calm connection that can follow. If you choose only one of these practices, I encourage you to choose this one, for it ultimately encompasses all of them.

Decide with care just what you want to put your attention to, and then do so. Whether it is the overall calm you are trying to achieve more of, a specific practice from this book that speaks to you, or perhaps just noticing when and where your child smiles during the day even in the midst of a challenging age or stage.

As you intentionally look for and pay attention to even a small thing in your day or with your child, you'll notice a few things. You'll notice yourself naturally relaxing. You'll discover more of what you are focusing on shows up—sometimes in surprising ways. You'll discover a greater awareness developing, a greater receptiveness to all that is happening. You'll find you are more curious, rather than critical or reactive. And this all leads to living PAUSE and growing your ability to let calm connection lead the way.

When my young teen daughter got sick multiple times every fall over a period of several years—interrupting school and the sports she lived for—I got increasingly worried. I wondered what was wrong, how I could prevent her from being sick, and how I could make her better. Despite all my efforts to "prevent her from being sick and make her better," she kept getting sick each fall. So I paused…and considered what I really wanted. Yes, for her to be healthy—but ultimately I wanted her to feel truly capable at managing her own health. I considered just what part of all this really was in my control and then decided to embrace the very thing I encouraged parents to do—to focus on what I wanted, *her being well*. Where I put my attention was something I could control.

You see, before I chose to intentionally focus on her wellness, I was (understandably!) truly wrapped up in how sick she was: looking for her cough getting worse, instead of finding where she seemed to rest most comfortably; waiting for the secondary infection signs, rather than recognizing how her body was keeping them at bay; keeping myself up half the night listening in case she might need me, instead of recognizing she was certainly old enough to let me know if she was miserable, as well as also getting the sleep I needed to be healthy throughout this! I was very busy helping her feel better, catering to her, making her comfortable, getting her to the doctor probably sooner than I really needed to, pursuing whatever I thought was necessary to "make her better." And yes, often things I pursued *were* necessary, like certain medications…but just as often I took steps that became totally unnecessary. We'd head to the doctor's office only to hear "She needs rest and extra fluids while the virus runs its course." Or I'd keep her home from school longer than necessary, or rush out to find the latest supplement that might be just the ticket to health. As I embraced "what we focus on grows," I shifted my focus to wellness—to how "being well" could look, even when sick. For my daughter, that meant focusing on where *she* took charge of her health during her illness—exactly what I truly wanted.

What did I do differently? I found I began interacting with her based on my confidence that she could manage her recovery and health well. Instead of catering to her, I began assuming she had already considered what she needed, so I'd ask her things like, "Before I head to the store, is there anything you need?" instead of, "Okay, I got you tissues, ibuprofen, a glass of water, and the movies you want to watch…" I began being a bit more matter-of-fact about her feeling crummy. "Looks like you are really congested. What do you need to help you?" instead of, "Ohhhh! Poor you. You look miserable. Here, have some…" I found I refocused on the things I usually do during the day, rather than on keeping her constant company or hovering nearby in case she might need something. I was still caring and concerned, but from a place of "I have confidence you know how to help yourself" rather than "You need me in order to get and be well." And I felt more relaxed and capable of seeing beyond illness to the daughter who often thrives with health. I began to sleep better, to only call the doctor when truly necessary, to notice what part of the days she did better, breathed easier, coughed less. I began to let calm connection lead the way, rather than the reactive and anxiety-driven "I've got to make her better!" mentality.

As a result, my daughter began to take increasing charge of herself, initially in subtle ways, such as remembering the box of tissues and helping herself to a glass of water, noticing what position really worked best for her to minimize her coughing, or asking me for something she needed. I spent less time hovering and catering, more time doing things with her that felt good to her. We found more time to play games, to knit, to bake (and eat!) the cookies she loves...☺ Over time, this translated to her working on being healthy during her usual get-sick times—intentionally getting more sleep, eating healthy foods, finding ways to relieve any stress she felt. Once she went off to college, my daughter had the confidence to seek her own medical help without constantly checking in with me. Instead of, "Mom! What do I do?" it was, "Mom, what more can I do? I've already tried...." Or "Oh, I was sick last week but now I'm up and running!"

The really cool thing was that she started spending her falls illness-free. And me? I definitely grew my ability to let calm connection lead the way in more of the struggles she faced—whether it was illness, injury, or other emotional duress. This calm connection—with myself and with her—allowed me to more easily "see" beyond the immediate struggle to the strong, healthy, independent young woman I knew was emerging. It allowed me to interact with her from a place of care, compassion, and confidence in HER abilities. What a powerful message to our children, when they feel our confidence in their journey. For my daughter and me, our relationship became even stronger in a wonderful way. I was a resource for her, and she was the capable and competent young woman I had kept my sight on. What a way to strengthen our ability to

PAUSE and let the power of calm connection permeate all we do. What a way to grow the kind of relationships we intend.

What you focus on grows. I encourage you to embrace this practice as a mantra to live by and notice what unfolds as a result. No matter how little of a step you take, how short a time something lasts, or how infrequently or briefly you can do something before losing it—it counts. Focus on what works. Focus on what you can appreciate about yourself, your child, your attempts at pausing and leading with calm connection. Focus on where your Best Self Qualities show up...where your child demonstrates the compassion, perseverance, and creativity you want them to have. Focus on the minute you set aside just for you, rather than your next eight hours of craziness. Keep your attention on being the calm, confident, positive influence your child needs the most. THIS is the power of PAUSE. **THIS is what can lead you to the power of parenting and living with calm connection.**

PAUSE

All that I'm doing to take PAUSE deeper...

Story Time!

Let's return to Tina and Katie and see how life looked as Tina took PAUSE deeper and let calm connection lead the way in all she did:

"Here we go again…" Tina smiled to herself as her twelve-year-old step-daughter, Katie, gave her The Silent Treatment on the way home from school—complete with The Eye Roll and even crossing her arms as she stared out the window. Tina silently chuckled to herself, remembering well doing the very same thing to her parents! "Tell me about your day!" was how she always greeted Katie, and sometimes all sorts of news spilled out, but other times—well, silence ☺. Tina respected Katie's need for space—a kind of PAUSE after a full day of school, which helped Katie regroup and (eventually) reconnect. Their fifteen-minute drive home was quiet, giving Tina time to reflect on what a productive day she had had with her employees—really enjoying the brainstorming sessions they'd had in an effort to move forward on a particularly difficult project. She found herself appreciating how others at work felt safe in coming to her, sharing their concerns, and feeling empowered as a result. "I so enjoy my work!" Tina smiled to herself.

The car door slammed as Katie continued The Silent Treatment, stomping off to her bedroom. "Wow," thought Tina. "She must've had a difficult day." Tina gathered up a much-needed snack for the both of them and headed to Katie's room, knocking and waiting for a response. "Come IN…" grumped Katie. Together they sat on the bed as Katie silently ate her snack and Tina, quietly to herself, made note of the disarray of schoolwork, the dirty laundry strewn across the floor, and even the dirty dishes from a previous snack. She was clear that now was not the time to encourage Katie to clean up a bit—that could be saved for another time.

After a few minutes of quiet companionship, out it poured: "I HATE school! The girls are so MEAN. I never want to go back!"

"Whew…It sounds like a bad day…" And Tina listened, lying down next to Katie, rubbing her back and letting her finish her

cry. It wasn't long until Katie sat back up, and together she and Tina talked about her day, how she felt, what she could do right now to feel better. Tina actually relished these times with Katie— it let her know that Katie really trusted and felt safe with her, and they always both ended up feeling closer. It was a lovely feeling!

A bit later, her husband, Mike, came home. Tina took him aside and let him know the struggles Katie had experienced at school that day. Mike listened, expressing his frustration over what seemed to him the disrespectful Silent Treatment Katie used. Tina's ability to PAUSE created a space for Mike to safely express his feelings—her quiet encouraged him to unload. His unloading helped Tina get a clearer picture of what Mike wanted—his daughter to fully embrace her as the new parent in her life. Understanding this helped Tina reassure Mike that Katie's and her relationship was truly beginning to blossom— that she felt confident in the direction they were going. Back and forth they continued as they sorted out together what was most important for Katie—and for Mike, as well. Eventually Mike headed into Katie's room to check in. Tina listened to their murmuring, knowing with certainty that Mike's time with their daughter would leave Katie feeling much, much better. Tina found her heart swelling a bit with this certainty—with the love she felt for both her husband and her stepdaughter.

Following what seemed like a lengthy time in the bedroom, Katie and Mike rejoined Tina. What a brainstorming session they had over dinner together! Katie shared some ideas she had for dealing with unkind girls at school; Tina and Mike offered up an assortment of activities to consider for their much-needed family time this weekend. Pretty soon they were all chuckling over some silly something, and as they cleared the dinner table, good humor seemed to rule. Following dinner, homework was tackled, Tina worked on her paperwork, and Mike took care of cleaning up the kitchen. It felt especially nice being together, each of them working on their own things, feeling comfortable and connected. The stress of work and family and life had, for now, subsided, and even though there was always more to be done and seemingly never enough time, Tina knew, without a doubt, that they would be okay—that they would continue to thrive!

This can be *your* story.

Taking PAUSE deeper and living the power of calm connection permeates all parts of your life, all of your relationships, everything. Being a practice, there is no "end goal" or "I'm there!" There are times of obvious strength and "Whew! I DID it. My pausing has made a real difference." There will be plenty of other times when you feel like you've taken many a step backwards as you find yourself caught up in another round of chaos. Know that your stronger pause muscle is now a part of the fabric of who you are, and nothing can change that. As with your self-care, every bit you do is a deposit—every bit you do strengthens this muscle. This does not mean the challenges of parenting and life will suddenly become pleasant—it means YOU are going to more likely step into them with the power of calm connection firmly on your side. And now you will discover how it can permeate all that you do, feel, and experience. How cool is that?

And, as with any practice, life gives you constant opportunity to do just this—practice. So PAUSE. Appreciate. Reframe. Use positive and affirming self-talk. Stay present to all your experiences. Focus on calm. Focus on connection. Gift yourself a do-over—mentally or in reality. Notice what is feeling better, what is working, where your Best Self Qualities step up. Pay attention to where you are letting calm connection weave its way through your day. Practice. And now your negative stories become positive ones, affirming ones, uplifting ones…ones you can appreciate, grow from, be grateful for. All because you started with a PAUSE. **What we focus on grows**.

Alice's Story

PAUSE Finds its Way...

I'm ending with one more story, one that maybe many of you can relate to and one that I hope will reinforce for you, yet again, the power that PAUSE and living with calm connection has as you let it lead the way in all you do.

While I wrote this book, I was going through a period of inner turmoil. I struggled to feel the balance, clarity, and confidence that PAUSE and the power of calm connection create in our lives. Here I was, writing all about the amazing relationship-building way of life PAUSE can be, and yet I was struggling to feel the calm connection from the inside out, struggling with relationships closest to me. I found doubt and confusion creep in. I asked myself how I could possibly write for you about the very thing that seemed lacking in my own life. But then something important happened...

I realized my sharing with you had me pausing and then appreciating the turmoil I felt. I found myself intentionally working on just what I've encouraged you to do...first working at actually welcoming in the turmoil, and then, because welcoming it in was just too difficult, I began just sitting still (in my mind, if not in reality) in my kind of PAUSE—a light-filled space in my mind's eye. I "sat." Waited. Listened. This was all I could do, off and on for several months. Wait. Listen. Sit in light. Write for you. Go back to waiting and listening. Yes, regular daily life went on around me just as usual—chaotic at times, fun often, full and busy always. But inside me? I was in conflict. Eventually this PAUSE of mine brought me to *allowing* my inner turmoil—**to being okay with it**. To finally welcoming it in and looking for the opportunities it offered (like some extra self-care defined by amazing dark chocolate and really awesome cups of coffee…). I found ways in which I could actually appreciate it, for I knew—without a doubt—that through this turmoil I could emerge stronger.

What did I discover? A deeper understanding and strengthening within me of what I want more of:

Trust. I strengthened my ability to trust life, to trust the universe, to trust myself and all the potential growth I knew this turmoil represented. This was huge—because trust really is the foundation for all that we do, for every life-affirming step we take as we live and grow. And when I can trust, I relax.

Letting Go. I allowed myself to let go of feeling a certain way, of being able to write authentically or write at all. To let go of trying to control just where my path was taking me and instead taking control of what I could—which was *how* I decided to respond to all the turmoil and feelings within. As I let go of trying to control all that was happening TO me, an amazing thing happened…I began to open myself to just being in the moment. To staying present to the turmoil, the upset, the stuff that was rocking my world a bit. And when I looked at these things carefully, when I appreciated what they offered, the turmoil began to calm.

Connection. I experienced real and meaningful connection—with myself, family, others I reached out to, and those who reached out to me…and even those I may have encountered only briefly during my day. I made real and meaningful connection with the critters in my life, the natural world around me, my spiritual self. This kind of connection always leaves me feeling a spring in my step and truly lifted.

Gratefulness. I began to feel grateful that I CAN feel so deeply, that I continue to have the opportunity to practice all that I write about and have it expand within me and out to others. I felt grateful for all the things in my life that are relationship-building. Grateful for daughters who share their love and support. Grateful for a husband who gives me the respect of time and space to sit…wait…listen.

And then calm connection—first within me, and then outside of me—showed up once again. The turmoil settled. Sometimes I forget what even stirred it up in the first place! I found it became easier to move through my days once again—smiles abundant, stress minimal. My thoughts settled and quieted themselves. I could "see" more clearly, my confidence resurged, I felt energized. A quiet confidence and joy once again defined my day. I felt lifted—ready to write, coach, parent, partner with my husband, create, change, be present, celebrate, cry, delight in things, be productive, contribute…BE all those things that define my Best Self.

And there it is—my Best Self reemerges even better. Calm connection rules—stronger this time for the balance has been tipped even more firmly on the side of just what I want more of.

What a practice this pausing is! The cool thing about this experience is that it reminds me yet again that turmoil is essential in order to live well. I know this, because each time I emerge from the turmoil with PAUSE leading the way, my relationships feel healthier, stronger, closer. I feel clearer in all that I am doing and intend to do. Calm and meaningful connection becomes the norm. It seems the more I get to practice PAUSE, the stronger I get. And the opportunities to practice it seem to keep on coming ☺.

This turmoil? It is worth every tear I shed and every bit of mad I felt and every shoulder I leaned on. I hope you will discover the same. Take your time. Allow any chaos or turmoil to have its place, for it is there to help you get better and better. Celebrate the simpler, easier, peaceful times of your life, and relish all your relationships. And know, without a doubt, that when turmoil defines life once again, you too can let it show you the gifts of growth it (eventually) offers. You can THRIVE.

All you really need to do is begin with a PAUSE.

With appreciation for each of you,

Alice

Acknowledgments

It is important to share with each of you the transformation I had as I incorporated my work as a PCI Certified Parent Coach® with *ScreamFree Parenting* by Hal Runkel. This book and all that I coach and live by extends from my growth as both a parent coach and ScreamFree Certified Leader. The work of Hal Runkel and Gloria DeGaetano (founder, Parent Coaching Institute) has changed my life—and the lives of many parents I've worked with—in subtle and profound ways. It is an honor and a privilege to bring this book to you to further and deepen the message that the Parent Coaching Institute and ScreamFree continue to share with all of us.

I am deeply appreciative for my writing and publishing consultant, Anne Dubuisson, for her guidance, encouragement, and celebration of my work throughout my entire writing process.

I give my heartfelt appreciation to my daughters and husband for all the opportunities they give me to practice parenting and living with the calm connection I intend. Without them, I would not have had the opportunity to experience firsthand all that I encourage and hope for in others.

And it is with deep gratitude to all the parents I've had the privilege of working with who have shared their trials, successes, and meaningful transformations with me as they, too, embrace PAUSE and the power of parenting and living with calm connection.

Thank you.

Alice Hanscam
PCI Certified Parent Coach®
ScreamFree Certified Leader

Endnotes

In the Beginning

[1] Pausing is a foundational piece to *ScreamFree Parenting: The Revolutionary Approach to Rising Your Kids by Keeping Your Cool*, by Hal Runkel. "The Power of Pause" phrase evolved through work with other PCI Certified Parent Coaches® and the ScreamFree Institute, www.screamfree.com.

[2] The concept of PAUSE being a muscle to strengthen comes from *ScreamFree Parenting*; Visit www.screamfree.com for more information.

PAUSE: The Power of Parenting (and Living) with Calm Connection

[1] Paraphrased from Hal Runkel and the ScreamFree Parenting CPR kit. Visit: http://screamfree.myshopify.com/collections/resources/products/screamfree-parenting-cpr for more information.

[2] To take control of ourselves is a key concept from *ScreamFree Parenting* and many other parenting resources for growing healthy and positive relationships.

[3] This concept of how control, influence, and healthy relationships are built has evolved from my work as a ScreamFree Certified Leader, a PCI Certified Parent Coach®, and my own personal experiences.

[4] "If you Live by the Remote, You Die by the Remote," *ScreamFree Parenting*, page 23.

PAUSE at Its Basic

[1] "What We Focus On Grows" is evolved from the Parent Coaching Institute's Living System Principles™, a part of the Parent Coach Certification® Training Program created by Gloria DeGaetano. Visit www.thepci.org for more information.

[2] The concept of self-care as a foundational piece to parenting and living well comes from many sources, as well as from personal experience. *Take Time for Your Life* by Cheryl Richardson, *ScreamFree Parenting*, and the Parent Coach Certification® Training Program created by Gloria DeGaetano for the Parent Coaching Institute have influenced me the most. There are many, many other resources showing the essential nature of caring first for ourselves.

[3] The emphasis on focusing first on yourself in order to calm down and respond rather than react is a key concept of and central to *ScreamFree Parenting*.

Taking PAUSE Deeper

[1] The concept of an "end in mind" can be found in *7 Habits of Highly Effective Families* by Stephen Covey and in *ScreamFree Parenting*, as well as in *Parenting Inspired; Finding Grace in the Chaos, Confidence in Yourself, and Gentle Joy along the Way*, by Alice Hanscam.

[2] Influenced by and evolved from *Dynamic Relationships: Unleashing the Power of Appreciative Inquiry in Daily Living* (p. 67), by Jacqueline Stavros and Cheri Torres, as well as from my work with Appreciative Inquiry (developed by David L. Cooperrider and explained in *Parenting Inspired*) in my coaching profession. Visit https://appreciativeinquiry.case.edu/ for more information.

Notes for myself to encourage me along...

What we focus on grows. I choose to focus on...

PAUSE made a real difference for me today by...

The power of calm connection is influencing all that I do by...

66947385R00064

Made in the USA
Charleston, SC
31 January 2017